POPULAR MECHANICS

HOME HOW-TO

WEATHERPROOFING
and
INSULATION

ALBERT JACKSON & DAVID DAY

HEARST BOOKS

This work has been extracted from *Popular Mechanics Home How-To* published by Hearst Books and created exclusively for William Collins Sons & Co. Ltd. by Jackson Day Jennings Ltd trading as Inklink.

Please note:
Great care has been taken to ensure the accuracy of the information in this book. However, in view of the complex and changing nature of building regulations, codes, and by-laws, the authors and publishers advise consultation with specialists in appropriate instances and cannot assume responsibility for any loss or damage resulting from reliance solely upon the information herein.

Library of Congress Cataloging-in-Publication Data

Jackson, Albert, 1943–
    Popular mechanics home how-to. Weatherproofing and insulation / Albert Jackson and David Day.
        p. cm.
    Includes index.
    ISBN 1-58816-078-5
    1. Dwellings—Insulation—Amateurs' manuals. 2. Waterproofing—Amateurs' manuals. I. Title: Weatherproofing and insulation. II. Day, David, 1944– III. Title.

TH1715 J22 2002
693.8'9.dc21   2001039115

Printed in Spain

Second Edition

1 2 3 4 5 6 7 8 9 10

CONTENTS

HOW TO USE THIS BOOK

This book has been written and designed to make finding information as easy as possible. **Running heads** identify the subjects covered on each page. **Tinted boxes** separate and highlight information related to the main text. **Headings** divide the main text into subsections so that you can easily locate specific information or a single stage in the work. **Cross-references** direct you to related information elsewhere in the book. The symbol ▷ next to a word indicates that the subject is discussed on another page. The specific cross-reference is listed in the margin of the page you're on. Cross-references printed in bold type are directly related to the task at hand. Those printed in lighter type will broaden your understanding of the subject.

ROUTINE MAINTENANCE

It sometimes seems that simply taking care of your home involves so much time and energy that it is difficult to even think about making substantial improvements. Indeed, maintenance of even a modest home involves looking after a rather complex system of structural, mechanical and decorative features.

But it is routine, methodical maintenance that prevents small problems from turning into large, expensive ones and that keeps a home running efficiently and economically. Attending to chores both inside and outside the home keeps what's already there intact and so provides the best opportunity for continuing improvement.

To keep maintenance tasks from seeming overwhelming, it's best to approach them on a seasonal basis. In most locales, spring and fall will be the busiest times as it seems best to take advantage of the moderate weather to repair damage from the extremes of the prior season and prepare for those of the upcoming one. The chart below suggests a schedule that would be appropriate for most regions of the country, and throughout the book you will find methods and measures for the various maintenance concerns discussed in greater detail.

SEASONAL MAINTENANCE SCHEDULE

WINTER

Doors and windows: Check for drafts and weatherstrip where necessary.
Heating system: Replace filters in forced-air systems once a month.
Fireplaces, stoves and chimneys: Clean and inspect flues in midseason.
Gutters, leaders and outdoor drains: Keep them clear of ice and debris.
Yard: Prune trees early to midseason.

SPRING

Roofing: Repair damaged shingles and flashing.
Gutters, leaders and outdoor drains: Clear debris and flush with water. Straighten and correct pitch of misaligned gutters. Reset leaders and tighten fasteners.
Siding and trim: Caulk and renail loose pieces. Restore failing paint. Wash all exterior surfaces.
Masonry: Repair cracks; repoint failing brick mortar joints.
Windows: Clean and unstick sash, repair damaged putty. Install insect screens in ventilating windows and shading devices on south-facing windows.
Pests: Check for termite and ant infestation. Check vent louvers, chimneys and other protective areas for bird and insect nests.
Heating system: Shut off unneeded appliances with standing pilots. Drain hydronic systems.
Fireplaces, stoves, and chimneys: Clean and inspect flues when seasonal use-period ends.
Air-conditioning equipment: Vacuum internal parts and clear drainage tubes.
Garden equipment: Clean and lubricate: fill oil reservoirs in gas-powered equipment and change air filters.

Lawn: Clear away accumulated leaves and debris. Test soil pH and amend as necessary. Dethatch, roll, and aerate; reseed as necessary. Apply preemergent weed killers and 25% of annual fertilizer allotment.

SUMMER

Air-conditioning equipment: Clean filters once monthly.
Mildew control: Clean away incipient growth with bleach solution; operate dehumidifiers in damp areas.
Lawn: Feed lawn with 50% of annual fertilizer allotment. Weed on a biweekly basis.

FALL

Gutters, leaders and outdoor drains: Clear debris and flush with water. Inspect joints and tighten brackets as necessary.
Heating system: Have equipment professionally serviced. Blow dust from thermostat contacts.
Air-conditioning equipment: Vacuum internal parts and wrap equipment.
Outdoor water supply: In frost-prone areas, shut off supply, drain lines and leave valves open.
Siding, trim and foundation: Patch and seal open cracks. Seal openings where animals may take refuge. Close vents of unheated crawlspaces.
Windows and doors: Put storm sash in place. Clean and repair screens, spray with protective coating before storing. Inspect and fortify weatherstripping. Clear debris from basement window wells.
Garden equipment: Drain fuel from gas engines. Clean metal surfaces and spray with protective coating.
Lawn: Clear leaves, dethatch and reseed.

KEEPING A CLEAN HOUSE

Regular cleaning of a home's exterior surfaces not only keeps them looking well-kept and attractive, it is an important aspect of preventive maintenance that can help stave off the need to refinish or replace materials on the outside of the home. We're not talking here about weekly scrubbings but only about taking a couple of hours once or twice a year to remove the buildup of grime and pollutants that can eat away at the skin of a home.

Even so-called no-maintenance materials such as vinyl and aluminum siding can benefit from a little care. Just dissolve 1 teaspoon of trisodium phosphate per gallon of water used, wash with a scrub brush and rinse with a garden hose.

TSP is also great for cleaning light soil from wood, painted surfaces and masonry. Household bleach will kill mildew and lift the dark stains. To remove heavy stains including mortar, efflorescence and paint from masonry, mix 1 part muriatic acid with 10 parts water and scrub with a wire brush. Lift grease and oil stains from concrete by sprinkling portland cement or corn starch over the area and wetting it with paint thinner or benzene. Keep the poultice moist for 24 hours, then rinse it away with clear water.

Weathered natural wood can be restored to its original color by scrubbing with oxalic acid solution. Kerosene is effective for removing rust stains and protecting steel screens.

Using a power washer
A power washer, which can be rented and attached to a garden hose, can be used to clean siding.

MOISTURE PROBLEMS: PRINCIPAL CAUSES

Dampness, or rather the symptoms of it, can be most distressing both in terms of your health and the condition of your home. Try to locate the source of the problem as quickly as possible before it promotes its even more damaging side effects—wet and dry rot. Unfortunately, one form of moisture problem may obscure another, or may appear in an unfamiliar guise. Moisture may enter a house either by wicking through from the outside or rising by osmosis from below. By a third method—condensation—moisture may form entirely within the house itself.

SEE ALSO

Details for:▷	
Damp-proof course	7
Wet and dry rot	11

Principal causes of penetrating moisture
1 Broken gutter
2 Leaking downspout
3 Missing shingle
4 Damaged flashing
5 Faulty pointing
6 Porous brick
7 Cracked masonry
8 Cracked stucco
9 Blocked drip groove
10 Defective seals around frames
11 Missing weatherstrip
12 Bridged cavity

Principal causes of rising moisture
Missing DPC or DPM
● Damaged DPC or DPM
● DPC too low
● Bridged DPC
● Earth piled above DPC

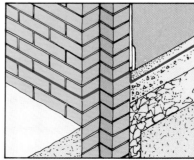

Penetrating dampness

Penetrating dampness is the result of water permeating the structure of the house from outside. The symptoms occur with wet weather only. After a few dry days, damp patches dry out but frequently leave stains.

Isolated patches are caused by a heavy deposit of water in one area and should pinpoint the source fairly accurately. General dampness usually indicates that the wall itself has become porous, but it could be caused by another problem.

Penetrating dampness occurs primarily in older homes with solid masonry walls. Relatively modern brick houses built with a cavity between two thinner brick skins are less likely to suffer from penetrating dampness, unless the cavity is bridged in one of several ways.

Rising dampness

Rising dampness is caused by water soaking up from the ground into the basement or slab floors, and walls of masonry houses. Most such houses are protected with an impervious barrier built into the walls and under concrete floors so that water cannot permeate above a certain level.

If the damp-proof course (DPC) in the walls or the damp-proof membrane (DPM) in a floor break down, water rises into the structure. Also, there may be something forming a bridge across the barrier so that water is able to flow around it.

Rising dampness is confined to solid floors and the lower sections of walls. It is a constant problem even in dry weather but becomes worse with prolonged wet weather.

DPC in a solid wall
A layer of impervious material is built into a joint between brick courses, 6 in. above the ground.

DPC and DPM in a cavity wall structure
The damp-proof membrane in a concrete floor is linked to the DPC protecting the inner leaf of the wall. The outer leaf has its own damp-proof course.

PENETRATING DAMPNESS: PRINCIPAL CAUSES

CAUSE	SYMPTOMS	REMEDY
Broken or blocked gutter Rainwater overflows the gutter, typically at the joints of old metal types, and saturates the wall directly below, so that it is prevented from drying out normally.	Damp patches appearing near the ceiling in upstairs rooms. Mold forming immediately behind the leak.	Clear leaves and silt from the gutters. Repair the gutters, or replace a faulty system with a maintenance-free plastic setup.
Broken or blocked downspouts A downspout that has cracked or rusted douses the wall immediately behind the leak. Leaves lodged behind the pipe at the fixing brackets will produce a similar effect eventually.	An isolated damp patch, often appearing halfway up the wall. Mold growth behind the pipe.	Repair or replace the defective downspout, using a maintenance-free plastic type. Clear the blockage.
Loose or broken roof shingles Defective shingles allow rainwater to penetrate the roof.	Damp patches appearing on upstairs ceilings, usually during a heavy downpour.	Replace the faulty shingles. Renew damaged roof parts, if necessary.
Damaged flashing Ridges, joints and seams in a roof are sealed with flashing strips. When the flashing cracks, peels or corrodes, water trickles down the wall or down the chimney stack.	Damp patches on the ceiling extending from the wall or chimney breast; also on the chimney breast itself. Damp patch on the side wall near roof joints or lean-to extension; damp patch on the lean-to ceiling itself.	Repair the existing flashing by refitting if it appears undamaged, or replace it.
Faulty pointing Aging mortar between bricks will eventually dry and fall out; water then penetrates the remaining jointing mortar to the inside of the wall.	Isolated damp patches or sometimes widespread dampness, depending on the extent of the deterioration.	Repoint the joints between bricks, then treat the entire wall with water-repellent fluid or paint.
Porous bricks Bricks in good condition are weatherproof, but old, soft bricks become porous and often lose their faces so that the whole wall is eventually saturated, particularly on an elevation that faces prevailing winds, or where some other drainage fault occurs.	Widespread dampness on the inner face of exterior sals. A noticeable increase in dampness during a downpour. Mold growth appearing on internal plaster and trim.	Weatherproof the exterior with a clear silicone fluid or exterior paint, or cement-stucco the surface where the deterioration is extensive.
Cracked brickwork A crack in a brick wall allows rainwater (or water from a leak) to seep inside, then run to the inside face.	An isolated damp patch, which may appear on a chimney breast if the stack is cracked.	Fill the cracks and replace any damaged brickwork.
Defective stucco Cracked or ruined stucco encourages rainwater to seep between it and the brick wall behind. The water is prevented from evaporating and so becomes absorbed by the wall.	An isolated damp patch, which may become widespread. The trouble can persist for some time after rain ceases.	Fill and reinforce the crack. Chip off the damaged stucco, patch it with new sand-cement stucco, then weatherproof the wall by applying exterior paint.
Damaged coping If the coping stone on top of a roof parapet wall is missing, or the joints are open, water can penetrate the wall.	Damp patches on the ceiling against the wall just below the parapet.	Bed a new stone on fresh mortar and repair the joints.

PENETRATING DAMPNESS: PRINCIPAL CAUSES

CAUSE	SYMPTOMS	REMEDY
Blocked drip groove Exterior windowsills should have a groove running longitudinally on the underside. When rainwater runs under, it falls off at the groove before reaching the wall. If the groove becomes bridged with layers of paint or moss, water will soak the walls behind.	Damp patches along the underside of a window frame. Rotting wooden sill on the inside and outside. Mold growth appearing on the inside face of the wall below the window.	Rake out the drip groove. Nail a wood or aluminum strip to the underside of a wooden sill to form a deflection for drips.
Failed seals around windows and door frames Timber frames shrink, pulling weatherstripping from around the edge so that rainwater can penetrate the gap.	Damp surrounding frames and rotting woodwork. Sometimes the gap itself is obvious where caulking has fallen out.	Repair the frames. Seal around the edge with fresh caulk.
No weatherstrip A weatherstrip across the bottom of a door should shed water clear of the threshold and prevent water from running under the door.	Damp floorboards just inside the door. Rotting at the base of the door frame.	Fit a weatherstrip even if there are no obvious signs of damage. Repair the frame.
Bridged wall cavity In a brick building, mortar dropped onto a wall tie connecting the inner and outer leaves of a cavity wall allows water to bridge the gap.	An isolated damp patch appearing anywhere on the wall, particularly after a heavy downpour.	Open up the wall and remove the mortar droppings, then waterproof the wall externally with paint or silicone repellent.

SEE ALSO

Details for: ▷

Drip molding	8
Sealing with caulk	8
Bridged cavity	8
Repairing frames	13-14, 23
Weatherstrip	21, 50-51
Waterproofing bricks	30

RISING DAMPNESS: PRINCIPAL CAUSES

CAUSE	SYMPTOMS	REMEDY
No DPC or DPM If a house was built without either a damp-proof course or damp-proof membrane, water is able to soak up from the ground.	Widespread dampness at the baseboard level. Damp concrete floor surface.	Fit a new DPC or DPM.
Broken DPC or DPM If either the DPC or DPM has deteriorated, water will penetrate at that isolated point.	Possibly isolated but spreading dampness at the baseboard level.	Repair or replace the DPC or DPM.
DPC too low The DPC may not be the necessary 6 inches above ground level. Heavy rain is able to splash above the DPC and soak the wall surface.	Dampness at baseboard level but only where the ground is too high.	Lower the level of the ground outside. If it's a path or patio, cut a 6-inch-wide trench and fill with gravel, which drains rapidly.
Bridged DPC Exterior stucco taken below the DPC, or fallen mortar at the foot of a cavity wall (within the cavity), allows moisture to cross over to the inside.	Widespread dampness at, and just above, baseboard level.	Chip off stucco to expose DPC. Remove several bricks and rake out debris from the cavity.
Debris piled against wall A flower bed, rock garden or area of paving built against a wall bridges the DPC. Building material and garden refuse left there will do likewise.	Dampness at baseboard level in the area of the bridge only, or spreading from that point.	Remove the earth or debris and allow the wall to dry out naturally.

DPC too low

Render bridges DPC

Earth piled over DPC

7

1 Water drips to ground

2 A bridged groove

3 Drip molding

Apply caulk with an applicator gun

CURING DAMPNESS

Remedies for different moisture problems are suggested throughout the Principal Causes boxes on the previous pages, and you will find detailed instructions for carrying out many of them in other sections of the book, where they contribute to other factors such as heat loss, poor ventilation, and spoiled interior and exterior finish. The information below supplements those instructions, by providing advice on measures solely to eradicate dampness.

WATERPROOFING WALLS

Applying a water repellent to the outside of a wall not only prevents water infusion but also improves insulation, reducing the possibility of interstitial condensation. This occurs when water vapor from inside the house penetrates the wall until it reaches the damp, colder part of the structure within the wall, where it condenses and eventually migrates back to the inner surface, causing stains and mold growth.

There are several vapor-proof liquids, including interior house paint, for painting on the inside of a wall, but they should be considered a temporary measure only, as they do not cure the source of the problem. Apply two full brush coats over an area appreciably larger than the extent of the dampness. Once the wall is dry, you can decorate it as required with paint or a wallcovering.

Alternatively, apply a waterproof laminate or paper. It is hung using standard wallpapering techniques with the manufacturer's own primer and adhesive. However, seams must be lapped by ½ inch to prevent moisture penetration.

PROVIDING A DRIP MOLDING

Because water cannot flow uphill, a drip molding on the underside of an external windowsill forces water to drip to the ground before it reaches the wall behind **(1)**. When painting, scrape the old paint or moss from the groove before it provides a bridge **(2)**.

You can add a drip molding to a wooden windowsill that does not have a precut drip groove by pinning and gluing a ¼-inch-square hardwood strip 1½ inches back from the front edge **(3)**. Paint or varnish the strip along with the windowsill.

SEALING AROUND WINDOW FRAMES

Scrape out old loose mortar or caulk from around the frame. Fill deep gaps with gap filler sold for the purpose, then seal all around with a flexible caulk. Caulk is available in cartridges to fit an applicator gun, or in tubes, which you squeeze just like toothpaste. Cut the end off the nozzle, then run it down the side of the frame to form a continuous, even bead. If the gap is very wide, fill it with a second bead when the first has set (follow directions). Most caulks form a skin and can be overpainted after a few hours, although they retain their waterproof characteristics even without being painted.

BRIDGED CAVITY

The simplest way to deal with a bridged wall cavity which allows water to flow to the inner leaf is to apply a water repellent to the outer surface.

However, this doesn't cure the cause, which may promote other moisture problems later. When it is convenient—when repointing perhaps—remove two or three bricks from the outside in the vicinity of the damp patch by chopping out the mortar around them. Use a small mirror and a flashlight to inspect the cavity. If you locate mortar lying on a wall tie, chip it off with a rod or opened metal coat hanger and replace the bricks.

Exposing a bridged wall tie
Remove a few bricks to chip mortar from a wall tie.

CONDENSATION

Air carries moisture as water vapor but its capacity depends on temperature. As it becomes warmer, air absorbs more water like a sponge. When water-laden air comes into contact with a surface that is colder than itself, it cools until it cannot any longer hold the water it has absorbed, and just like the sponge being squeezed, it condenses, depositing water in liquid form onto the surface.

Conditions for condensation

The air in a house is normally warm enough to hold water without reaching the saturation point, but a great deal of moisture is also produced by members of the household using baths and showers, cooking and even breathing. In cold weather when the low temperature outside cools the external walls and windows below the temperature of the heated air inside, all that extra water runs down window panes and soaks into the wallpaper and plaster. Matters are made worse in the winter by sealing off windows and doors so that fresh air cannot replace humid air before it condenses.

Dampness in a fairly new house which is in good condition is almost certainly due to condensation.

The root cause of condensation is rarely simple, as it is a result of a combination of air temperature, humidity, lack of ventilation and thermal insulation. Tackling one of them in isolation may transfer condensation elsewhere or even exaggerate the symptoms. However, the box opposite lists major contributing factors to the total problem.

Condensation appears first on cold glazing

CONDENSATION: PRINCIPAL CAUSES

CAUSE	SYMPTOMS	REMEDY
Insufficient heat The air in an unheated room may already be close to the point of saturation. (Raising the temperature increases the ability of the air to absorb moisture without condensing.)	General condensation.	Heat the room (but not with a kerosene heater, which produces moisture).
Kerosene A kerosene heater produces as much water vapor as the fuel it burns, and condensation will form on windows, walls and ceilings.	General condensation in the room where the heater is used.	Substitute another form of heating.
Uninsulated walls and ceilings Moist air readily condenses on cold exterior walls and ceilings.	Widespread dampness and mold. The line of ceiling joists is picked out as mold grows less well along these relatively "warm" spots.	Install attic insulation.
Cold bridge Even when a wall has cavity insulation, there can be a cold bridge across the window frames and studs in contact with both exterior and interior walls.	Damp patches or mold surrounding the window frames.	Try painting walls with vapor-barrier paint. If necessary, attach polyethylene vapor barrier over the inside wall, then cover with paneling.
Uninsulated pipes Cold water pipes attract condensation. It is often confused with a leak when water collects and drips from the lowest point of a pipe run.	Line of dampness on a ceiling or wall following the pipework. Isolated patch on a ceiling, where water drops from plumbing. Beads of moisture on the underside of a pipe.	Insulate the plumbing with fiberglass wrapping.
Cold windows Glass shows condensation usually before any other surface, due to the fact that it's very thin and constantly exposed to the elements.	Misted glass, or water collecting in pools at the bottom of the window pane.	Double-glaze the window. If condensation occurs inside a secondary glazing system, place some silica gel crystals (which absorb moisture) in the cavity between panes.
Sealed fireplace When a fireplace opening is blocked, the air trapped inside the flue cannot circulate and consequently condenses on the inside, eventually soaking through the brickwork.	Damp patches appearing anywhere on the chimney breast.	Ventilate the chimney by inserting a grille at a low level in the blocked-up part of the fireplace.
Attic insulation blocking airways If attic insulation blocks the spaces around the eaves, air cannot circulate in the roof space, and condensation is able to form.	Widespread mold affecting the timbers in the roof space.	Unblock the airways and, if possible, fit a ventilator grille in the soffit.
Condensation on recent building If you have carried out work involving new bricks, mortar and especially plaster, condensation may be the result of these materials exuding moisture as they dry out.	General condensation affecting walls, ceilings, windows and solid floors.	Wait for the new work to dry out, then review the situation, before decorating or otherwise treating.

DAMP-PROOFING A CELLAR

Being at least partially below ground level, the walls and floors of a cellar or basement invariably suffer from dampness to some extent. If the problem cannot be tackled from the outside—usually most effective—you will have to seal out the moisture by treating the internal surfaces. Rising dampness in concrete floors, whatever the situation, can be treated as described below, but penetrating or rising dampness in walls other than in a cellar should be cured at the source. Merely sealing the internal surface encourages the dampness to penetrate elsewhere eventually. Also make sure a treated cellar is properly ventilated, and even heated to avoid condensation problems in the future.

Treating the floor

If you are laying a new concrete floor, incorporate a moisture barrier during its construction. If the barrier was omitted or has failed in an existing floor, seal the floor with a heavy-duty, moisture-curing polyurethane.

Preparing the surface
The floor must be clean and grease-free. Fill any cracks and small holes by priming with one coat of urethane, then one hour later apply a mortar made from 6 parts sand: 1 part cement plus enough urethane to produce a stiff paste. Although urethane can be applied to damp or dry surfaces, it will penetrate a dry floor better, so force-dry excessively damp basements with a fan heater before treatment. Remove all heaters from the room before you begin damp-proofing.

Applying urethane
Use a broom to apply the first coat of urethane using the coverage recommended by the manufacturer. If you are treating a room with a damp-proof barrier in the walls, take the urethane coating up behind the baseboard to meet it.

Two or three hours later, apply a second coat. Further delay may result in poor intercoat adhesion. Apply three or four coats in all.

After three days, you can lay any conventional floorcovering or use the floor as it is.

PATCHING ACTIVE LEAKS

Before you damp-proof a cellar, patch cracks which are active water leaks (running water) with a quick-drying hydraulic cement. Supplied as a powder for mixing with water, the cement expands as it hardens, sealing out the running water.

Undercut a crack or hole with a chisel and club hammer. Mix up cement and hold it in your hand until warm, then push it into the crack. Hold it in place with your hand or a trowel for three to five minutes until hard.

TREATING THE WALLS

If you want, you can continue with moisture-cured polyurethane to completely seal the walls and floor of a cellar. Decorate with latex or oil paints within 24 to 48 hours after treatment for maximum adhesion.

If you'd prefer to hang wallpaper, apply two coats of latex paint first and use a heavy-duty paste. Don't hang impervious wallcoverings such as vinyl, however, as it's important that the wall be able to "breathe."

Bitumen latex emulsion
Where you plan to sheetrock the basement walls, you can seal out dampness with a cheaper product, bitumen latex emulsion. It is not suitable as an unprotected covering to walls or floors, although it is often used as an integral damp-proof membrane (DPM) under the top layer of a concrete floor and as a waterproof adhesive for some tiles and wooden parquet flooring.

Chip off old plaster, if necessary, to expose the brickwork, then apply a skim coat of mortar to smooth the surface. Paint the wall with two coats of bitumen emulsion, joining with the DPM in the floor. Attach furring strips to the coated wall using construction adhesive, then install plasterboard.

Cement-based waterproof coating
In severe conditions, use a cement-based waterproof coating. Chip off old plaster or stucco to expose the wall. Then, to seal the junction between a concrete floor and the wall, cut a groove about ¾ inch wide by the same depth. Brush out the debris and fill the channel with hydraulic cement (see left), finishing it off neatly as an angled fillet.

Mix the powdered cement-based coating to a butterlike consistency, according to the manufacturer's instructions, then apply two coats to the wall with a bristle brush.

However, when brick walls are damp, they bring salts to the surface in the form of white crystals known as effloresence, so before treating with waterproof coating, apply a salt-inhibiting stucco consisting of 1 part sulphate-resisting cement: 2 parts clean rendering sand. Add 1 part liquid bonding agent to 3 parts of the mixing water. Apply a thin troweled coat to a rough wall or brush it into a relatively smooth surface and allow it to set.

Treating a wall with bitumen latex emulsion
1 Skim coat of mortar
2 Coat of bitumen latex
3 Furring strips
4 Plasterboard

Moisture-curing polyurethane
Damp-proof a floor with three or four coats of urethane applied with a broom.

WET AND DRY ROT

Rot occurs in unprotected household timbers, fences and outbuildings, which are subjected to dampness. Fungal spores, which are always present, multiply and develop in these conditions until eventually the timber is destroyed. Fungal attack can be serious, requiring immediate attention to avoid very costly structural repairs to your home. There are two main scourges: wet and dry rot.

Recognizing rot

Signs of fungal attack are easy enough to detect but it is important to be able to identify certain strains which are much more damaging than others.

Mold growth
White, furry deposits or black spots on timber, plaster or wallpaper are mold growths; usually these are a result of condensation. When they are wiped or scraped from the surface, the structure shows no sign of physical deterioration apart from staining. Cure the source of the damp condition and treat the affected area with a solution of 16 parts warm water: 1 part bleach.

Wet rot

Wet rot occurs in timber with a high moisture content. As soon as the cause is eliminated, further deterioration is arrested. Wet rot frequently attacks the framework of doors and windows which have been neglected, enabling rainwater to penetrate joints or between brickwork and adjacent timbers. Peeling paintwork is often the first sign, which when removed reveals timber that is spongy when wet but dark brown and crumbly when dry. In advanced stages, the grain will have split and thin, dark brown fungal strands will be in evidence on the timber. Treat wet rot as soon as practicable.

Dry rot

Once it has taken hold, dry rot is a most serious form of decay. Urgent treatment is essential. It will attack timber with a much lower moisture content than wet rot, but—unlike wet rot, which thrives outdoors as well as indoors—only in poorly ventilated, confined spaces indoors.

Dry rot exhibits different characteristics depending on the extent of its development. It sends out fine, pale gray tubules in all directions, even through masonry, to seek out and infect other drier timber. It actually pumps water from damp timber and can progress at an alarming rate. The strands are accompanied by white cotton woollike growths, called mycelium, in very damp conditions. When established, dry rot develops wrinkled, pancake-shaped fruiting bodies, which produce rust-red spores that are expelled to rapidly cover surrounding timber and masonry. Infested timbers become brown and brittle, exhibiting cracks across and along the grain until it breaks up into little cubes. You may also detect a strong, musty, mushroomlike smell associated with the fungus.

Wet rot—treat it as early as possible

Dry rot—urgent treatment is essential

TREATING ROT

Dealing with wet rot
After eliminating the cause of the dampness, cut away and replace badly damaged wood, then paint the new and surrounding woodwork with three liberal applications of fungicidal wood preservative. Brush the liquid well into the joints and end grain.

Before decorating, you can apply a penetrating epoxy wood hardener to reinforce and rebuild damaged timbers, then repaint as normal.

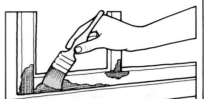

Fill rotted timbers with epoxy wood hardener

Dealing with dry rot
Dry rot requires more drastic action and should be treated by a specialist contractor, unless the outbreak is minor and self-contained. Remember that dry rot can penetrate masonry. Look under the floorboards in adjacent rooms before you are satisfied with the extent of the infection; check cavity walls for signs of rot.

Eliminate the source of water and ensure adequate ventilation in roof spaces or under the floors. Cut out all infected timber up to at least 1 foot 6 inches beyond the last visible sign of rot. Chop plaster from nearby walls, following the strands. Continue for another 1 foot 6 inches beyond the extent of the growth. Collect all debris in plastic bags and burn it or dispose of it away from the property.

Use a fungicidal preservative fluid to kill remaining spores. Wire-brush the masonry, then apply three liberal brush-coats to all timber, brickwork and plaster within 5 feet of the infected area. Alternatively, rent a sprayer and go over the same area three times.

If a wall was penetrated by strands of dry rot, drill regularly spaced but staggered holes into it from both sides. Angle the holes downwards so that fluid will collect in them to saturate the wall internally. Patch holes after treatment.

Treat replacement timbers and immerse the end grain in a bucket of fluid for five to ten minutes. If you are repairing a plaster eall, apply a zinc-oxychloride plaster.

ROT: PREVENTATIVE TREATMENT

Fungal attack can be so damaging that it is well worth taking precautions to prevent its occurrence. Regularly repaint and maintain window and door frames, where moisture can penetrate; seal around them with silicone caulk. Provide adequate ventilation between floors and ceilings; do the same in the attic. Check and eradicate any plumbing leaks and other sources of dampness, and you'll be less likely to experience the stranglehold rot can apply.

Looking after timberwork

Existing and new timbers can be treated with a preservative. Brush and spray three applications to standing timbers, paying particular attention to joints and end grain.

Immersing timbers

Timber in contact with the ground should be completely immersed in preservative. Stand fence posts on end in a bucket of fluid for 10 minutes. For other timbers, make a shallow bath from loose bricks and line it with thick polyethylene sheet. Pour preservative into the trough and immerse the timbers, weighing them down with bricks (1). To empty the bath, sink a bucket at one end of the trough, then remove the bricks adjacent to it so the fluid pours out (2), or use a bulb-type hand pump to suck up the liquid.

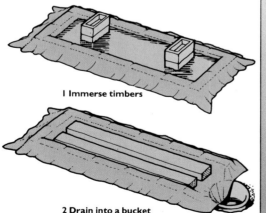

1 Immerse timbers

2 Drain into a bucket

WOOD PRESERVATIVES

Wood exposed to moisture should be treated with preservative to prevent rot. There are numerous types of wood preservatives, so be sure you choose the correct one for the timber you want to protect.

LIQUID PRESERVATIVES

For treatment of existing indoor and outdoor wood, choose a liquid preservative that you can apply by soaking or with a brush. Although all wood preservatives are toxic, the safest are copper and zinc napthenate, as well as copper-8-quinolinolate, tributyltin oxide (TBTO) and polyphase. Avoid using the traditional creosote or pentachlorophenol (penta). These chemicals are known carcinogens and highly toxic. If the wood must come into direct ground contact, use copper napthenate. Liquid preservatives, which are often sold as preservative stains, are readily available from paint stores, lumberyards and building supply stores.

PRESSURE-TREATED LUMBER

Consider using pressure-treated lumber for new outdoor construction and where wood will come in contact with ground or concrete. Use lumber stamped LP-22 for contact with soil; wood stamped LP-2 is only for above-ground use. Inhaling chemicals used to treat lumber can be harmful, so wear a mask when sawing and don't burn scraps.

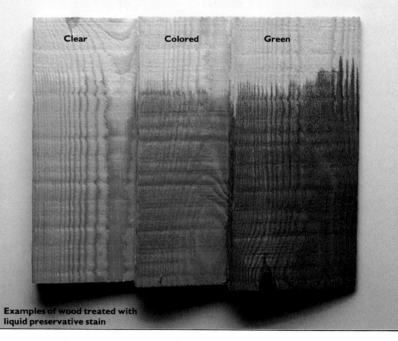

Clear   Colored   Green

Examples of wood treated with liquid preservative stain

SAFETY WITH PRESERVATIVES

All preservatives are flammable, so do not smoke while using them, and extinguish open flames.

Wear protective gloves at all times when applying preservatives and wear a face mask when using these liquids indoors.

Ensure good ventilation when the liquid is drying, and do not sleep in a freshly treated room for two nights to allow the fumes to dissipate fully.

WINDOWS: REPAIRING ROTTED FRAMES

Softwood is the traditional material for making wooden window frames, and providing it is of sound quality and is well cared for, it will last the life of the building.

Regular maintenance

It is the bottom rail of a wooden window frame that is most vulnerable to rot if it is not protected. The water may be absorbed by the wood through a poor paint finish or by penetrating behind old shrunken putty. An annual check of all window frames should be

New frames or frames that have been stripped should always be treated with a clear wood preservative before being primed and painted.

carried out and any faults should be dealt with. Old putty that has shrunk away from the glass should be cut out and replaced.

Remove old, flaking paint, repair any cracks in the wood with a flexible filler and repaint, ensuring that the underside of the sash is well painted.

Replacing a sash rail

Where rot is well advanced and the rail is beyond repair, it should be cut out and replaced. This should be done before the rot spreads to the stiles of the frame. Otherwise you will eventually have to replace the whole sash frame.

Remove the sash either by unscrewing the hinges or—if it is a double-hung sash window—by removing the beading.

With a little care the repair can be carried out without the glass being removed from the sash frame, though if the window is large it would be safer to take out the glass. In any event, cut away the putty from the damaged rail.

The bottom rail is tenoned into the stiles (1), but it can be replaced by using bridle joints. Saw down the shoulder lines of the tenon joints (2) from both faces of the frame and remove the rail.

Make a new rail, or buy a piece if it is a standard section, and mark and cut it to length with a full-width tenon at each end. Set the positions of the tenons to line up the mortises of the stiles. Cut the shoulders to match the rabbeted sections of the stiles (3) or, if it has a decorative molding, pare the molding away to leave a flat shoulder (4).

Cut slots in the ends of the stiles to receive the tenons.

Glue the new rail into place with a waterproof resin adhesive and reinforce the two joints with pairs of ¼-inch dowels. Drill the stopped holes from the inside of the frame and stagger them for greater rigidity.

When the adhesive is dry, plane the surface as required and treat the new wood with a clear preservative. Reputty the glass and paint the new rail within three weeks.

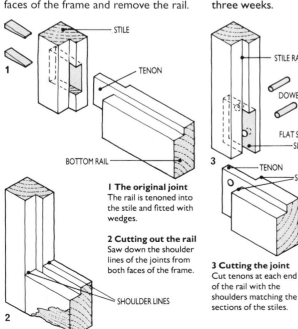

1 The original joint
The rail is tenoned into the stile and fitted with wedges.

2 Cutting out the rail
Saw down the shoulder lines of the joints from both faces of the frame.

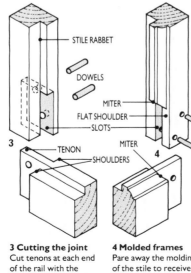

3 Cutting the joint
Cut tenons at each end of the rail with the shoulders matching the sections of the stiles.

4 Molded frames
Pare away the molding of the stile to receive the square shoulder of the rail. Miter the molding.

REPLACING A FIXED-LIGHT RAIL

The frames of some fixed lights are made like sashes but are screwed to the main frame jamb and mullion. Such a frame can be repaired in the same way as a sash (see left) after its glass is removed and it is unscrewed from the window frame. Where this proves too difficult, you will have to carry out the repair in place.

First remove the putty and the glass, then saw through the rail at each end. With a chisel, trim the rabbeted edge of the jamb(s) and/or mullion to a clean surface at the joint (1) and chop out the old tenons. Cut a new length of rail to fit between the prepared edges and cut mortises in its top edge at both ends to take loose tenons. Place the mortises so that they line up with the mortises in the stiles and make them twice as long as the depth of those mortises.

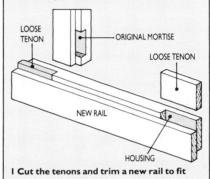

1 Cut the tenons and trim a new rail to fit

Cut two loose tenons to fit the rail mortises, and two packing pieces. The latter should have one sloping edge (2).

Apply waterproof woodworking adhesive to all of the joint surfaces, place the rail between the frame members, insert the loose tenons and push them sideways into the stile mortises. Drive the packing pieces behind the tenons to lock them in place. When the adhesive has set, trim the top edges, treat the new wood with clear preservative, replace the glass and reputty. Paint within three weeks.

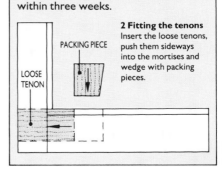

2 Fitting the tenons
Insert the loose tenons, push them sideways into the mortises and wedge with packing pieces.

SEE ALSO

Details for: ▷	
Removing glass	18

● **Removing glass**
Removing glass from a window frame in one piece is not easy, so be prepared for it to break. Apply adhesive tape across the glass to bind the pieces together if it should break. Chisel away the putty to leave a clean rabbet, then pull out the points. Work the blade of a putty knife into the bedding joint on the inside of the frame to break the grip of the putty. Steady the glass and lift it out when it becomes free.

REPAIRING ROTTED SILLS

The sill is a fundamental part of a window frame, and one attacked by rot can mean major repair work.

A window frame is constructed in the same way as a door frame and can be repaired in a similar way. All the glass should be removed first, preferably by removing the sashes. Be sure to check the condition of the subsill (part of the rough frame). Rot can extend into this region also if the opening was not covered with building paper. After repairs have been made, be careful to thoroughly weatherseal the window frame to prevent moisture from entering once again. Reapply fresh 15-pound asphalt-saturated building paper around exposed parts of the rough frame, then caulk all seams where the window frame itself contacts the exterior of the house. Repairing sills is difficult and time-consuming, so plan to do such work during warm weather when window openings can be covered with polyethylene while work progresses.

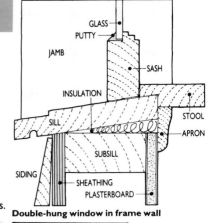

Double-hung window in frame wall

Replacing a wooden sill

Ideally, to replace a rotted window sill you should remove the entire window, carefully disassemble the old sill from the jamb sides, use it as a template, then cut and fit a new sill and replace the window. However, sills may be replaced with the window in place, provided you work patiently and have some skill at scribing and shaping wood with a chisel. Begin by carefully splitting out the old sill. Cut through it crosswise in two places with a saw to remove the middle portion, then gently pry the end sections away from the jambs. Hacksaw any nails holding the sill to the rest of the frame.

Use a piece of cardboard to make a template for a new sill, shaped to fit between the jambs but beneath the casing on the outside. Cut a 10-degree bevel along the upper outside edge of the sill, extending to the inside edge of the sash, then bevel the sash area so it is level when the sill is installed. Fill the area beneath the sill with insulation, install the sill with 16d finishing nails, then thoroughly caulk the seams.

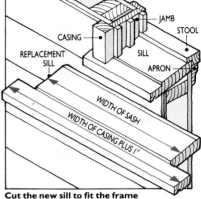

Cut the new sill to fit the frame

Repairing a stone subsill

The traditional stone sills featured in older houses may become eroded by the weather if they are not protected with paint. They may also suffer cracking due to subsidence in part of the wall.

Repair any cracks and eroded surfaces with a quick-setting waterproof cement. Rake the cracks out to clean and enlarge them, then dampen the stone with clean water and work the cement well into the cracks, finishing off flush with the top surface.

Depressions caused by erosion should be undercut to provide the cement with a good hold. A thin layer of cement simply applied to a shallow depression in the surface will not last. Use a cold chisel to cut away the surface of the sill at least 1 inch below the finished level and remove all traces of dust.

Make a wooden form to the shape of the sill and temporarily nail it to the brickwork. Dampen the stone, pour in the cement and tamp it level with the form, then smooth it with a trowel. Leave it to set for a couple of days before removing the form. Let it dry thoroughly before painting.

Make a wooden form to the shape of the sill

CASTING A NEW SUBSILL

Cut out the remains of the old stone sill with a hammer and cold chisel. Make a wooden mold with its end pieces shaped to the same section as the old sill. The mold must be made upside down, its open top representing the underside of the sill.

Fill two thirds of the mold with fine ballast concrete, tamped down well, and then add two lengths of mild steel reinforcing rod, judiciously spaced to share the volume of the sill, then fill the remainder of the mold. Set a narrow piece of wood such as a dowel into notches previously cut in the ends of the mold. This is to form a "throat" or drip groove in the underside of the sill.

Cover the concrete with polyethylene sheeting or dampen it regularly for two or three days to prevent rapid drying. When the concrete is set (allow about seven days), remove it from the mold and re-lay the sill in the wall on a bed of mortar to meet the wooden sill.

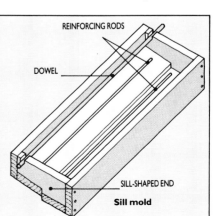

Sill mold

Frame walls

Most new windows today are prefabricated and set into place as a single unit. Installing them is similar to installing doors.

First, measure the rough opening to be sure it is large enough to accept the window. Then, sheath all four sides of the opening with 15-pound building paper to prevent moisture damage (**1**). Set the window into the opening from outside. Center it, then raise it on shims from the inside to the specified height.

Set a level on top of the sill and adjust the shims until the frame is both plumb and horizontal. From outside, carefully drive one finishing nail into an upper corner of the casing, partway into a stud. Start a nail in the opposite corner, check that the window frame is level, and drive the nail through the casing into the stud.

Measure between diagonal corners of the frame to be sure it is square, then insert shims between the side jambs to hold it in position. Nail the lower corners in place carefully (**2**). After rechecking the frame for squareness, plumb and level, operate the sashes. If no further adjustment is necessary, finish nailing, trim shims flush, pack insulation between the window frame and rough opening from the inside, install a drip cap above the window, and caulk all seams to exclude moisture (**3**).

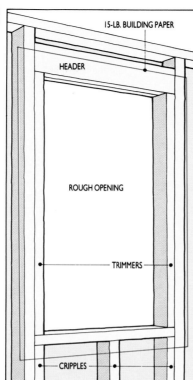

1 Be sure opening matches window
To narrow an opening, install extra trimmers or strips of plywood. Widen an opening by adding a new stud next to the framed opening and removing a trimmer. Alter the height of an opening by rebuilding the sill and lower cripples, not the header.

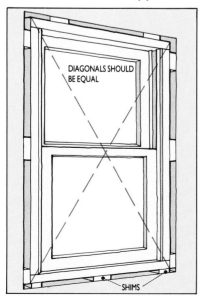

2 Tack window in place
Adjust with shims until all measurements are satisfactory and sash operates smoothly. Measurements taken between diagonals will be exactly equal if frame is square.

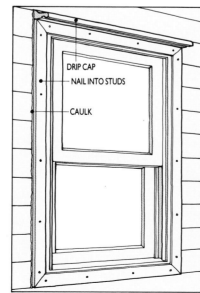

3 Nail through casing into studs only
Do not nail into sheathing. If necessary, pre-drill holes to prevent splitting. Attach drip cap to top of casing. Fill all nail holes with putty. Apply caulk around all four sides.

Masonry walls

In older brick houses it is usual to find the window frame jambs set in recesses on the inside of the brickwork. The openings were formed before the windows were fitted and the frames were nailed or screwed into wooden plugs in the brickwork. No vertical damp-proof courses were fitted. Evaporation was relied on to keep the walls dry.

The frames in a 9-inch-thick wall were set flush with the inside. Thicker walls had inner reveals. All required sub-sills, usually stone ones, outside.

Brickwork above the opening in a traditional brick wall may be supported by a brick arch or a stone lintel. Flat or shallow curved arches were generally used, their thickness being the width of one brick. Wooden lintels were placed behind such arches to support the rest of the wall's thickness. Semi-circular arches were usually as thick as the wall.

Many stone lintels were carved to make decorative features. As with arches, an inner lintel shared the weight. Openings like this were never wide because of the relative weakness of the materials. The wide windows of main rooms had several openings divided by brick or stone columns.

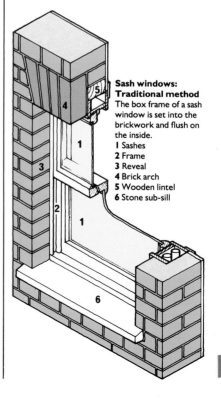

Sash windows: Traditional method
The box frame of a sash window is set into the brickwork and flush on the inside.
1 Sashes
2 Frame
3 Reveal
4 Brick arch
5 Wooden lintel
6 Stone sub-sill

BUYING GLASS

You can buy most types of glass from building supply and hardware stores. They will advise you on thickness, cut the glass to your measurements and also deliver larger sizes and amounts.

The thickness of glass, once expressed by weight, is now measured in inches. If you are replacing old glass, measure its thickness to the nearest 32nd, and, if it is slightly less than any available size, buy the next one up for the sake of safety.

Though there are no regulations about the thickness of glass, for safety reasons you should comply with the recommendations set out in the Uniform Building Code or your local code. The required thickness of glass depends on the area of the pane, its exposure to wind pressure and the vulnerability of its situation—e.g., in a window overlooking a play area. Tell your supplier what the glass is needed for—a door, a window, a shower screen, etc.—to ensure that you get the right type.

Measuring

Measure the height and width of the opening to the inside of the frame rabbet, taking the measurement from two points for each dimension. Also check that the diagonals are the same length. If they differ markedly and show that the frame is out of square, or if it is otherwise awkwardly shaped, make a cardboard template of it. In any case deduct 1/8 inch from the height and width to allow a fitting tolerance. When making a template allow for the thickness of the glass cutter.

When you order patterned glass, specify the height before the width. This will ensure that the glass is cut with the pattern running in the right direction. (Or take a piece of the old glass with you, which you may need to do in any case to match the pattern.)

For any asymmetrically shaped pane of patterned glass supply a template, and mark the surface that represents the outside face of the pane. This ensures that the glass will be cut with its smooth surface outside and will be easier to keep clean.

WORKING WITH GLASS

Always carry glass on its edge. You can hold it with pads of folded rag or paper to grip the top and bottom edge, though it is better to wear heavy working gloves.

Protect your hands with gloves and your eyes with goggles when removing broken glass from a frame. Wrap up the broken pieces in thick layers of newspaper if you have to dispose of them in your wastebasket, but before doing so check with your local glazier, who may be willing to take the pieces and add them to his cut-offs, to be sent back to the manufacturers for recycling.

Basic glass-cutting

It is usually unnecessary to cut your own glass as glass suppliers are willing to do it, but you may have surplus glass and want to cut it yourself. Diamond-tipped cutters are available, but the type with a steel wheel is cheaper and adequate for normal use.

Cutting glass successfully is largely a matter of practice and confidence. If you have not done it before, you should make a few practice cuts on waste pieces of glass and get used to the "feel" before doing a real job.

Lay the glass on a flat surface covered with a blanket. Patterned glass is placed patterned side down and cut on its smooth side. Clean the surface thoroughly.

Set a T-square the required distance from one edge, using a steel measuring tape (1). If you are working on a small piece of glass or do not have a T-square, mark the glass on opposite edges with a felt-tip pen or wax pencil. Use a straight edge to join up the marks and guide the cutter.

Lubricate the steel wheel of the glass cutter by dipping it in light machine oil or kerosene. Hold the cutter between middle finger and index finger (2) and draw it along the guide in one continuous stroke. Use even pressure throughout and run the cut off the end. Slide the glass forward over the edge of the table (3) and tap the underside of the scored line with the back of the cutter to initiate the cut. Grip the glass on each side of the score line with gloved hands (4), lift the glass and snap it in two. Alternatively, place a pencil under each end of the scored line and apply even pressure on both sides until the glass snaps.

1 Measure the glass with a tape and T-square

2 Cut glass in one continuous stroke

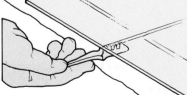

3 Tap the edge of glass to initiate the cut

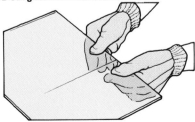

4 Snap glass in two

Cutting a thin strip of glass

A pane of glass may be slightly oversize due to inaccurate measuring or cutting or if the frame is distorted.

Remove a very thin strip of glass with the aid of a pair of pliers. Nibble away the edge by gripping the waste with the tip of the jaws close to the scored line.

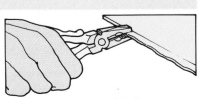

Nibble away a thin strip with pliers

Fitting items such as an extractor fan may involve cutting a circular hole in a pane of glass. This can be done with a beam compass cutter.

Cutting a circle in glass

Locate the suction pad of the central pivot on the glass, set the cutting head at the required distance from it and score the circle around the pivot with even pressure (**1**). Now score another smaller circle inside the first one. Remove the cutter and score across the inner circle with straight cuts, then make radial cuts about 1 inch apart in the outer rim. Tap the center of the scored area from underneath to open up the cuts (**2**) and remove the inner area. Next tap the outer rim and nibble away the waste with pliers if necessary.

To cut a disc of glass, scribe a circle with the beam compass cutter, then score tangential lines from the circle to the edges of the glass (**3**). Tap the underside of each cut, starting close to the edge of the glass.

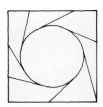

1 **Score the circle with even pressure**

2 **Tap the center of the scored area**

SEE ALSO

Details for:▷	
Repairing broken windows	18
Glass cutter	77

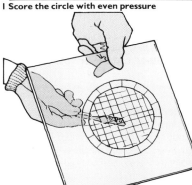

3 **Cutting a disc**
Scribe the circle then make tangential cuts from it to the edge of the glass.

Smoothing the edges of cut glass

You can grind down the cut edges of glass to a smooth finish using wet-and-dry sandpaper wrapped around a wooden block. It is fairly slow work, although just how slow will depend on the degree of finish you require.

Start off with medium-grit paper wrapped tightly around the wood block. Dip the block complete with paper in water and begin by removing the "arris" or sharp angle of the edge with the block held at 45 degrees to the edge. Keep the abrasive paper wet.

Follow this by rubbing down the vertical edge to remove any nibs and go on to smooth it to a uniform finish. Repeat the process with progressively finer grit papers. A final polish can be given with a wet wooden block coated with pumice powder.

● **Plastic glazing**
As an alternative to glass for awkward shapes you can use acrylic plastic, cutting it with a fret saw.

Using a glass-cutting template

Semi-circular windows and glazed openings in Georgian-style doors are formed with segments of glass set between radiating glazing-bars.

Windows with semi-circular openings and modern reproductions of period doors can be glazed with ready-shaped panes available from building suppliers, but for an old glazed door you will probably have to cut your own. The pieces are segments of a large circle, beyond the scope of the beam compass glass cutter (see above), so you will have to make a cardboard template.

Remove the broken glass, clean up the rabbet, then tape a sheet of paper over the opening and, using a wax crayon, take a rubbing of the shape (**1**). Remove the paper pattern and tape it to a sheet of thick cardboard. Following the lines on the paper pattern, cut the card to shape with a sharp knife, but make the template about ¹/₁₆ inch smaller all around, also allowing for the thickness of the glass cutter. The straight cuts can be aided by a straightedge, but you will have to make curved ones freehand. A slightly wavy line will be hidden by the frame.

Fix the template to the glass with double-sided tape, score around it with the glass cutter (**2**), running all cuts to the edge, and snap the glass in the normal way.

1 **Take a rubbing of the shape with a crayon**

2 **Cut around the template**

Drilling a hole in glass

There are special spear-point drilling bits available for drilling holes in glass. As glass should not be drilled at high speed, use a hand-held wheel brace.

Mark the position for the hole, no closer than 1 inch to the edge of the glass, using a felt-tipped pen or a wax pencil. On mirror, glass work from the back or coated surface.

Place the tip of the bit on the marked center and, with light pressure, twist it back and forth so that it grinds a small pit and no longer slides off the center. Form a small ring with putty around the pit and fill the inner well with a lubricant such as kerosene or water.

Work the drill at a steady speed and with even pressure. Too much pressure can chip the glass.

When the tip of the drill just breaks through, turn the glass over and drill from the other side. If you drill straight through from one side, you risk breaking the surface around the hole.

Drilling glass
Always run the drill in a lubricant to reduce friction.

REPAIRING A BROKEN WINDOW

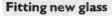

A cracked window pane, even when no glass is missing from it, is a safety hazard and a security risk. If the window is actually lacking some of its glass, it is no longer weatherproof and should be repaired promptly.

Temporary repairs

For temporary protection from the weather, a sheet of polyethylene can be taped or pinned with strips over the outside of the window frame, and a cracked window can be temporarily repaired with a special clear self-adhesive waterproof tape. Applied to the outside, the tape gives an almost invisible repair.

Safety with glass

The method you use to remove the glass from a broken window will to some extent depend on conditions. If the window is not at ground level, it may be safest to take out the complete sash to do the job. But a fixed window will have to be repaired on the spot, where it is.

Large pieces of glass should be handled by two people and the work done from a scaffold rather than ladders. Avoid working in windy weather and always wear protective gloves for handling glass.

Repairing glass in wooden frames

In wooden window frames the glass is set into a rabbet cut in the frame's molding and bedded in linseed-oil putty. Small wedge-shaped nails called glazier's points are also used to hold the glass in place. In some wooden-framed windows a screwed-on beading is used to hold the pane instead of the "weathered" (outer) putty; this type of frame may have its rabbet cut on the inside instead of the outside.

Removing the glass

If the glass in a window pane has shattered, leaving jagged pieces set in the putty, grip each piece separately (wearing gloves) and try to work it loose (**1**). It is safest always to start working from the top of the frame.

Old dry putty will usually give way, but if it is strong it will have to be cut away with a glazier's hacking knife and a hammer (**2**). Alternatively, the job can be done with a blunt wood chisel. Work along the rabbet to remove the putty and glass. Pull out the points with pincers (**3**).

If the glass is cracked but not shattered, run a glass cutter around the perimeter of the pane about 1 inch from the frame, scoring the glass (**4**). Fasten strips of self-adhesive tape across the cracks and the scored lines (**5**) and tap each piece of glass so that it breaks free and is held only by the tape. Carefully peel the inner pieces away, then remove the pieces around the edges and the putty as described above.

Clean out the rabbet and seal it with a wood primer. Measure the height and width of the opening to the inside of the rabbets and have your new glass cut ⅛ inch smaller on each dimension to give a fitting tolerance.

Fitting new glass

Purchase new glazier's points and enough putty for the frame. Your glass supplier should be able to advise you on this but, as a guide, 1 pound of putty will fill about 13 linear feet.

Knead a palm-sized ball of putty to an even consistency. Very sticky putty is difficult to work with so wrap it briefly in newspaper to absorb some of the oil. You can soften putty that is too stiff by adding linseed oil to it.

Press a fairly thin, continuous band of putty into the rabbet all around with your thumb. This is the bedding putty. Lower the edge of the new pane on to the bottom rabbet, then press it into the putty. Press close to the edges only, squeezing the putty to leave a bed about ¹⁄₁₆ inch behind the glass, then secure the glass with points about 8 inches apart. Tap them into the frame with the edge of a firmer chisel so that they lie flat with the surface of the glass (**1**). Trim the surplus putty from the back of the glass with a putty knife.

Apply more putty to the rabbet all around, outside the glass. With a putty knife (**2**), work the putty to a smooth finish at an angle of 45 degrees. Wet the knife with water to prevent it dragging and make neat miters in the putty at the corners. Let the putty set and stiffen for about three weeks, then apply an oil-based undercoat paint. Before painting, clean any putty smears from the glass with paint remover. Let the paint lap the glass slightly to form a weather seal.

A self-adhesive plastic foam can be used instead of the bedding putty. Run it around the back of the rabbet in a continuous strip, starting from a top corner, press the glass into place on the foam and secure it with points. Then apply the weathered putty in the same way described above. Alternatively, apply a strip of foam around the outside of the glass and cover it with a wooden beading, then paint.

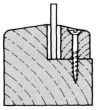

Weathered putty

Wooden bead
Unscrew beading and scrape out mastic. Bed new glass in fresh astic and replace beading.

1 Work loose the broken glass

2 Cut away the old putty

3 Pull out the old points

4 Score glass before removing a cracked pane

5 Tap the glass to break it free

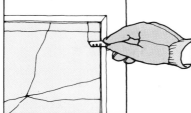

1 Tap in new points

2 Shape the putty

READY-MADE WINDOWS

Building suppliers offer a range of ready-made window frames in wood, vinyl and aluminum, and some typical examples are shown below.

Unfortunately, the range of sizes is rather limited, but where a ready-made frame is fairly close to one's requirements, it is possible to alter the size of the window's rough opening by cutting out or adding frame pieces, as described on page 198. In a wall of exposed brickwork, the window frame should be made to measure.

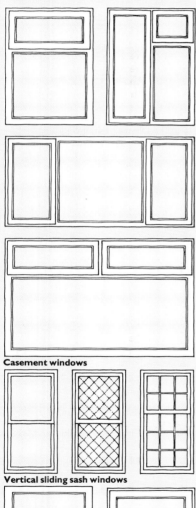

Casement windows

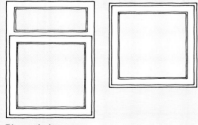

Vertical sliding sash windows

Pivot windows

REPLACEMENT WINDOWS

The style of the windows is an important element in the appearance of any house. Should you be thinking of replacing windows in an older dwelling you might find it better—and not necessarily more expensive—to have new wooden frames made rather than to change to modern windows of aluminum or vinyl.

Planning and building regulations

Window conversions do not normally need planning permission, as they come under the heading of home improvement or home maintenance. But if you plan to alter your windows significantly—for example, by bricking one up or making a new window opening, or both—you should consult your local building inspector.

All codes have certain minimum requirements, some pertaining to ventilation and some to the ratio of glass area to floor space.

You should also find out from your local authority if you live in a historic section, which could mean some limitation on your choice.

Buying replacement windows

Custom woodworking mills will make up wooden window frames to your size. Specify hardwood or, for a painted finish, softwood impregnated with a preservative.

Alternatively, you can approach one of the replacement window companies, though this is likely to limit your choice to aluminum or vinyl frames. The ready-glazed units can be fitted to your present framing or to new framing, should alteration be necessary. Most of the replacement window companies operate on the basis of supplying and also fitting the windows, and their service includes disposing of the old windows after removal.

This method saves time and labor, but you should carefully compare the various offerings of these companies and their compatibility with the style of your house before opting for one. Choose a frame that reproduces, as closely as possible, the proportions of the original window.

Replacing a casement window

Measure the width and height of the window opening. Windows in brick masonry will need a wood subframe. If the existing one is in good condition, take your measurements from inside the frame. Otherwise, take them from the brickwork. You may have to cut away some of the stucco first to get accurate measurements. Order the replacement window accordingly.

Remove the old window by first taking out the sashes and then the panes of glass in any fixed part. Unscrew the exposed hardware, such as may be found in a metal frame, or pry the parts of the frame out and cut through fasteners with a hacksaw. It should be possible to knock the frame out in one piece, but if not, saw through it in several places and lever the pieces out with a crowbar (1). Clean up the exposed masonry with a bricklayer's chisel to make a neat opening.

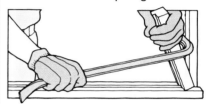

1 Lever out the pieces of the old frame

Cut the horns off the new frame if present, then plumb the frame in the window opening and wedge it (2). Drill screw holes through the stiles into the rough frame or masonry (3). Refit the frame, checking again that it is plumb before screwing it home.

Patch the wall on both sides if necessary. Gaps of ¼ inch or less can be filled with caulk. Glaze the new frame as required.

2 Fit the new frame **3 Drill screw holes**

SEE ALSO

Details for: ▷
Fitting windows   15

19

DOORS: FITTING AND HANGING

Whatever the style of door you wish to fit, the procedure is the same, though minor differences between some exterior doors may show themselves. Two good-quality 4-inch butt hinges are enough to support a standard door, but if you are hanging a heavy hardwood door, you should add a third, central hinge.

All doors are fairly heavy, and as it is necessary to try a door in its frame several times to get the fit right, you will find that the job goes much more quickly and easily if you have a helper working with you.

Fitting a door

Before attaching the hinges to a new door, make sure that it fits nicely into its frame. It should have a clearance of ¹⁄₁₆ inch at the top and sides and should clear the floor by at least ¹⁄₄ inch. As much as ¹⁄₂ inch may be required for a carpeted floor.

Measure the height and width of the door opening and the depth of the rabbet in the door frame into which the door must fit. Choose a door of the right thickness and, if you cannot get one that will fit the opening exactly, one which is large enough to be cut down.

Cutting to size
Transfer the measurements from the frame to the door, making necessary allowance for the clearances all around. To reduce the width of the door, stand it on edge with its latch stile upwards while it is steadied in a portable vise. Plane the stile down to the marked line, working only on the one side if a small amount is to be taken off. If a lot is to be removed, take some off each side. This is especially important with panel doors to preserve the symmetry.

If you need to take off more than ¹⁄₄ inch to reduce the height of the door, remove it with a saw and finish off with a plane. Otherwise, plane the waste off (**1**). The plane must be sharp to deal with the end grain of the stiles. Work from each corner towards the center to avoid "chipping out" the corners. If you must trim a panel door by more than 4 inches, remove the waste entirely from the bottom. Then refit the spline in the exposed channel.

Try the door in the frame, supporting it on shallow wedges (**2**). If it still doesn't fit, take it down and remove more wood where appropriate.

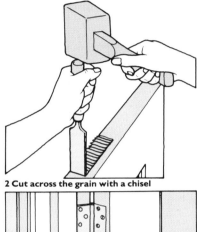

Plane to size

Wedge the door

Fitting hinges

The upper hinge is set about 7 inches from the door's top edge and the lower one about 10 inches from the bottom. They are cut equally into the stile and door frame. Wedge the door in its opening and, with the wedges tapped in to raise it to the right floor clearance, mark the positions of the hinges on both the door and frame.

Stand the door on edge, the hinge stile uppermost, open a hinge and, with its knuckle projecting from the edge of the door, align it with the marks and draw around the flap with a pencil (**1**). Set a marking gauge to the thickness of the mortise. Chisel out a series of shallow cuts across the grain (**2**) and pare out the waste to the scored line. Repeat the procedure with the second hinge, then, using the flaps as guides, drill pilot holes for the screws and fix both hinges into their mortises.

Wedge the door in the open position, aligning the free hinge flaps with the marks on the door frame. Make sure that the knuckles of the hinges are parallel with the frame, then trace the mortises on the frame (**3**) and cut them out as you did the others.

Adjusting and aligning
Hang the door with one screw holding each hinge and see if it closes smoothly. If the latch stile rubs on the frame, you may have to make one or both mortises slightly deeper. If the door strains against the hinges, it is what is called "hinge bound." In this case, insert thin cardboard strips beneath the hinge flaps to shim them out and retest door operation. When the door finally opens and closes properly, drive in the rest of the screws.

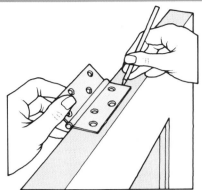

I Mark around the flap with a pencil

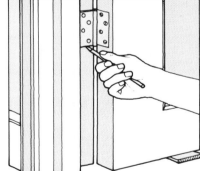

2 Cut across the grain with a chisel

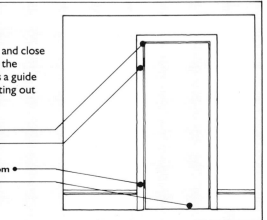

3 Mark the size of the flap on the frame

MEASUREMENTS

A door that fits well will open and close freely and look symmetrical in the frame. Use the figures given as a guide for trimming the door and setting out the position of the hinges.

¹⁄₈-in. clearance at top and sides ●
Upper hinge 7 in. from the top ●

Lower hinge 10 in. from the bottom ●
¹⁄₄- to ¹⁄₂-in. gap at the bottom ●

CLEARING THE FLOOR/WEATHERSTRIPPING A DOOR

Rising butt hinges

Rising butt hinges lift a door as it is opened and are fitted to prevent it from dragging on thick pile carpet.

They are made in two parts: a flap, with a fixed pin, which is screwed to the door frame, and another, with a single knuckle, which is fixed to the door, the knuckle sliding over the pin.

Rising butt hinges can be fastened only one way up, and are therefore made specifically for left- or right-hand opening. The countersunk screwholes in the fixed-pin flap indicate the side to which it is made to be fitted.

Fitting

Trim the door and mark the hinge positions (see opposite), but before fitting the hinges, plane a shallow bevel at the top outer corner of the hinge stile so that it will clear the frame as it opens. As the stile runs through to the top of the door, plane from the outer corner towards the center to avoid splitting the wood. The top strip of the door stop will mask the bevel when the door is closed.

Fit the hinges to the door and the frame, then lower the door onto the hinge pins, taking care not to damage the molding above the opening.

ADJUSTING BUTT HINGES

Perhaps you have a door catching on a bump in the floor as it opens. You can, of course, fit rising butt hinges, but the problem can be overcome by resetting the lower hinge so that its knuckle projects slightly more than the top one. The door will still hang vertically when closed, but as it opens the out-of-line pins will throw it upwards so that the bottom edge will clear the bump.

Resetting the hinge
You may have to reset both hinges to the new angle to prevent binding.

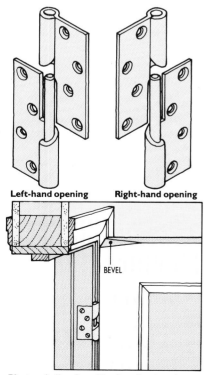

Left-hand opening   **Right-hand opening**

BEVEL

Plane a shallow bevel to clear the door frame

Weatherstripping a door

Weatherstripping is special molding fitted to the bottom of an exterior door to prevent moisture and the flow of air underneath. Many styles are available. Some require that the door be trimmed, some do not. Often, weatherstripping comes as an integral part of the threshold itself, and is easily installed merely by screwing the threshold to the sill.

When installing a new door, consider attaching a type of weatherstrip which mounts to the bottom of the door or to the threshold directly beneath it. When retrofitting weatherstripping, a style that attaches to the inside of the door at its lower edge is easier to apply, and adjustable as well.

Weatherstripping that flexes or is walked on will wear out in time. It is a good idea to check its condition each year and replace it if necessary. The best time to do this is *before* the onset of inclement weather.

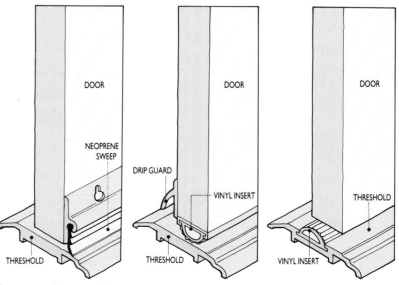

Three types of door weatherstripping

21

INSTALLING A PRE-HUNG DOOR

Purchasing a door already attached to a matching frame saves a great deal of time and permits even novice DIYers to accomplish accurate work. Install the side of the door frame to which the door is attached first, by inserting it in the rough opening (1), wedged from below to allow clearance above finish flooring. Trim the lower ends of the jamb sides if necessary (2), then center the frame within the opening and align it horizontally and vertically using a level and plumb bob. Anchor the frame in place by shimming out the sides and head jamb with shims (3). Use finishing nails to fasten the shims securely to the frame and rough opening. Also drive finishing nails through the door casing into the edges of the rough opening members. If the door frame is the split-jamb type that adjusts to fit different wall thicknesses, complete the installation by attaching the other half of the frame into the rough opening from the other side (4).

SEE ALSO

◁ Details for:
Hanging doors   20

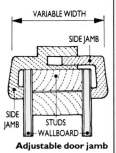
VARIABLE WIDTH

SIDE JAMB

SIDE JAMB

STUDS

WALLBOARD

Adjustable door jamb

JAMB   CASING

ROUGH OPENING

1 Install door

WEDGES

FINISH FLOOR

2 Trim with saw

DOOR

SHIMS

ROUGH OPENING

JAMB

3 Shim out jambs

CASING

JAMB

4 Attach remaining casing

REPAIRING EXTERIOR DOOR FRAMES

Exterior door frames are built into the brickwork as it is erected, so replacing an old one means some damage to the plaster or the outside stucco.

In older houses, the frames are recessed into the brickwork, the inside face of the frame is flush with the plaster work and the architrave covers the joint. Modern houses may have frames close to or flush with the outer face of the brickwork. Work from the side the frame is closest to.

Measure the door and buy a standard frame to fit, or make one from standard frame sections.

Removing the old frame

Chop back the plaster or stucco with a chisel to expose the back face of the door frame (1).

With a general-purpose saw (2) cut through the three metal brackets holding the frame in the brickwork on each side, two about 9 inches from the top and bottom and one halfway up.

Saw through the jambs halfway up (3), and if necessary cut the head member and the sill. Lever the frame members out with a crowbar.

Clear any loose material from the opening and repair a vertical vapor barrier in a cavity wall with gun-applied caulking to keep moisture out of the gap between inner and outer layers of brickwork.

Fitting the new frame

Fitting a frame is easier with its horns removed, but this weakens it. If possible, fit the frame with horns shaped like the old ones (see right).

Wedge the frame in position, checking that it is centered, square and plumb. Drill three counterbored clearance holes in each jamb for screws, positioned about 1 foot from the top and bottom with one halfway, but avoid drilling into mortar joints. Run a masonry drill through the clearance holes to mark their position on the brickwork.

Remove the frame, drill the holes in the brickwork and insert expandable metal wall plugs. Replace the frame and fix it with 4-inch steel screws. Plug the counterbores.

Pack any gap under the sill with mortar. Restore the brickwork, stucco or plasterwork and apply mastic sealant around the outer edge of the frame to seal any small gaps. Fit the door as described (◁).

1 Cut back to expose the back of the frame

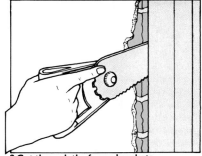
2 Cut through the frame brackets

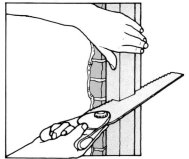
3 Saw through the frame to remove it

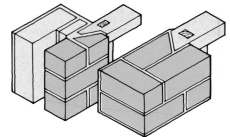
Shape the horns rather than cut them off

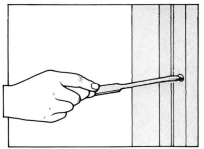
Screw the frame to the plugged wall

REPLACING A ROTTED FRAME

The great majority of exterior door frames are constructed of softwood, and this, if it is regularly maintained with good paint, will give years of excellent service. However, the ends of door sills and the frame posts are vulnerable to rot if they are subject to continual wetting. This can happen when the frame has moved because of shrinkage of the timber, or where old pointing has fallen out and left a gap where water can get in. Alternatively, old and porous brickwork or an ineffective moisture barrier can be the cause of moisture damage.

Prevention is always better than any cure, so check around the frame for any shrinkage gaps and apply a mastic sealant where necessary. Keep all pointing in good order. A slight outbreak of rot can be treated with the aid of a commercial repair kit and preservative.

Replacing a sill

You can buy 2 × 6 softwood or hardwood door sill sections that can be cut to the required length. If your sill is not of a standard-shaped section, the replacement can be made to order. It is more economical in the long run to specify a hardwood such as oak, as it will last much longer.

Taking out the old
First measure and note down the width of the door opening, then remove the door. Old jamb sides are usually tenoned into the sill, so to separate the sill from them, split it lengthwise with a wood chisel. A saw cut across the center of the sill can make the job of removing it easier.

The ends of the sills are set into the brickwork on either side, so cut away the bricks to make the removal of the old sill and insertion of the new one easier. Use a cold chisel to cut carefully through the mortar around the bricks, and try to preserve them for reuse after fitting the sill.

The new sill has to be inserted from the front so that it can be tucked under the jamb sides and into the brickwork. Cut the tenons off level with the shoulders of the jamb sides (1). Mark and cut shallow mortises for the ends of the jamb sides in the top of the new sill, spaced apart as previously noted. The mortises must be deep enough to take the full width of the jamb sides (2), which may mean the sill being slightly higher than the original one, so that you will have to trim a little off the bottom of the door.

Fitting the new
Try the new sill for fit and check that it is level. Before fastening it, apply a wood preservative to its underside and

It is possible for the sill to rot without the frame posts being affected. In this case, all you have to do is replace the sill. If the posts are also affected, repair them (see right). In some cases, the post ends can be tenoned into the sill and fitted as a unit.

ends, and, as a moisture barrier, apply two or three coats of asphalt roofing sealer to the brickwork.

When both treatments are dry, glue the sill to the jamb sides, using an exterior woodworking adhesive. Wedge the underside of the sill with slate to push it up against the ends of the sides, toenail the sides to the sill and leave it for the adhesive to set.

Pack the gap between the underside of the sill and the masonry with a stiff mortar of 3 parts sand : 1 part cement, and rebond and point the bricks. Finish by treating the wood with preservative and applying a caulking sealant around the door frame.

1 Cut tenons off level with the joint's shoulder

2 Cut a mortise to receive the side

REPAIRING DOOR POSTS

Rot can attack the ends of door posts, particularly in exposed positions where they meet stone steps or are set into concrete, as is found in some garages. The posts may be located on metal dowels set into the step.

If the damage is not too extensive, the rotted end can be cut away and replaced with a new piece, either scarf-jointed or half-lap-jointed into place. If your situation involves a wooden sill, combine the following information with that given for replacing a sill.

First remove the door, then saw off the end of the affected post back to sound wood. For a scarf joint, make the cut at 45 degrees to the face of the post (1). For a lap joint, cut it square. Chip any metal dowel out of the step with a cold chisel.

Measure and cut a matching section of post to the required length, allowing for the overlap of the joint, then cut the end to 45 degrees or mark and cut a half lap joint in both parts of the post (2).

Drill a hole in the end of the new section for the metal dowel if it is still usable. If it is not, make a new one from a piece of galvanized steel pipe, priming the metal to prevent corrosion. Treat the new wood with a preservative and insert the dowel. Set the dowel in mortar, at the same time gluing and screwing the joint (3).

If a dowel is not used, fix the post to the wall with counterbored screws. Place hardboard or plywood shims behind it if necessary and plug the counterbores of the screw holes.

Apply a caulk sealant to the joints between the door post, wall and base.

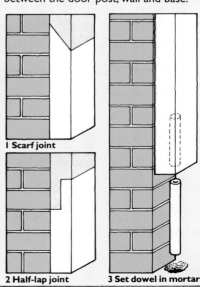

1 Scarf joint

2 Half-lap joint **3 Set dowel in mortar**

REPAIRING A CONCRETE FLOOR

Filling a crack

Clean all dirt and loose material out of the crack and, if necessary, open up narrow parts with a cold chisel to allow better penetration of the filler.

Prime the crack with a solution of 1 part bonding agent : 5 parts water and let it dry. Make a filler of 3 parts sand : 1 part cement mixed with equal parts of bonding agent and water; or use a ready-mixed quick-setting cement. Apply the filler with a trowel, pressing it well into the crack.

Foundation drainage

There are several techniques for draining perpetually wet basements. One is to dig a 1- to 2-foot-deep sump pit at one spot in the floor, near a corner if possible. Line the sides of the pit with a section of sewer tile and spread a 2- to 4-inch layer of gravel in the bottom. Install a sump pump to get rid of the water as it accumulates. Another method, to be installed before pouring a new floor, is to lay pipe in a slanting trench dug downward beneath the house footing. Digging under the footing is easier than drilling through a foundation wall; however, if the footings are located several feet below the level of the slab, it might make more sense to drill through the wall instead. Install a floor drain at the high end and connect the low end to the exterior foundation drain, or direct it into the gravel base around the footing. Fill in the trench, then pour the floor, sloping the surface toward the drain opening.

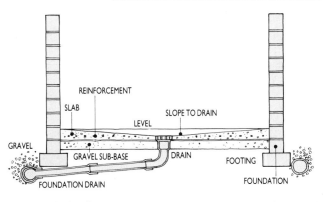

Sump pump details

OUTLET LINE
SUMP PUMP
SLAB
INTAKE
GRAVEL
FLOAT-SWITCH

Floor drain details

REINFORCEMENT
SLAB
LEVEL
SLOPE TO DRAIN
GRAVEL
GRAVEL SUB-BASE
DRAIN
FOOTING
FOUNDATION
FOUNDATION DRAIN

RESURFACING CONCRETE FLOORS

Only in severe cases must a concrete slab floor be rebuilt. Have a concrete engineer or building inspector assess major cracking or other deterioration, but if the surface is spalled (flaked due to expanding moisture during freezing weather), chipped or even moderately cracked, and the floor is well supported, a new layer of concrete may be poured over the top and smoothed to a new finish relatively easily.

Preparing the surface

The first step is to clean and roughen the floor to provide good bonding for the new layer. Thoroughly sweep the surface and remove loose material from cracks. With a hammer and chisel, score shallow grooves in the floor, just deep enough to expose the coarse material below the finish surface. Consider renting a scarifying machine or a jack hammer if the floor is large. Scrub oil stains on the floor with a strong industrial detergent and rinse thoroughly with water to get rid of slick film.

Next, it is a good idea to etch the surface with hydrochloric or muriatic acid to ensure bonding. Commercial preparations containing these, especially for the purpose, are available at building supply centers. Make sure there is plenty of ventilation, and always wear a respirator, goggles, rubber boots and gloves. Spread the solution with a long-handled push broom. After the acid stops foaming, hose down the floor with plenty of water and scrub it with a clean broom. Remove all acid residue.

Setting forms

Most resurfacing doesn't require forms; the perimeter walls are usually adequate. However, in order to level the surface, you must install strips of wood whose top edges can serve as guides for screeding (see diagrams). Depending on the particular circumstances, you can either lay a double row of long strips running the entire length of the floor, or you can pour the concrete in 2-foot-wide bands, using only a single strip as a guide after the first pour has hardened. After each band is poured and screeded, relocate the board 2 feet further on and continue the process.

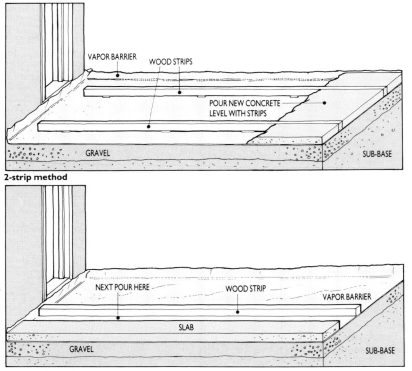

VAPOR BARRIER
WOOD STRIPS
POUR NEW CONCRETE LEVEL WITH STRIPS
GRAVEL
SUB-BASE

2-strip method

NEXT POUR HERE
WOOD STRIP
VAPOR BARRIER
SLAB
GRAVEL
SUB-BASE

Single-strip method

CONCRETE FLOORS

Pouring

If the new floor will be more than 2 inches thick, cut and have ready squares of wire-mesh reinforcement to place between layers of concrete. Begin the actual pour by spreading a ⅛-inch layer of bonding grout (1 part cement/1 part sand/½ part water) over the prepared surface using a stiff push broom. Then, while the grout is still wet, immediately spread on the concrete, mixed 1 part cement/1 part sand/2 parts ⅜-inch-diameter crushed stone. Use a square-nose shovel to distribute the mix. When the layer is 1 inch thick, lay down the mesh if required, then spread the remaining concrete over it.

Spread grout with broom

Shovel on concrete

Screeding

Use a straight 2 × 4 laid across the embedded wood strips to level the poured concrete. Work the board back and forth with a sawing motion while simultaneously drawing it along the length of the strips. When you are finished, carefully remove the strips while kneeling on wide boards laid on the concrete to distribute your weight, fill in the troughs with concrete, and smooth with a wood float.

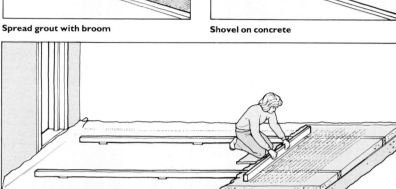

Level concrete with straightedge. Lift out and fill hollows left by strips

Floating and troweling

For a smooth-textured finish floor, work a wood float over the surface of the slab once the concrete is strong enough to bear your weight but is still soft enough to take an imprint. Concrete ready for floating has a frosted appearance. Small floats are available at hardware stores. Make or rent a long-handled one if space allows. For large floors, consider renting a gasoline-powered float. Lay two squares of plywood on the floor to kneel on. The boards should not sink more than ¼ inch into the concrete.

Later, when the concrete will bear no imprint, polish the surface with a steel trowel for a smooth, hard finish suitable as a base for carpet or other soft flooring. Do not trowel a floor that will be left bare. When wet it may become dangerously slick. Trowel the concrete only until it is smooth. Over-troweling causes the particulate matter in the concrete to sink, and the cement to rise, and later flake. Cover the finished concrete with plastic sheeting for a week or so to let it cure without drying out. Afterward, apply a masonry sealer.

Smooth the surface with a float

Polish nearly cured concrete with steel trowels

MIXING CONCRETE

You can rent small mixing machines if you have to prepare a large volume of concrete, but for the average job it is just as convenient to mix concrete by hand. It isn't necessary to weigh out the ingredients when mixing concrete. Simply mix them by volume, choosing the proportions that suit the job at hand.

• **Professional mixing**
There are companies who will deliver concrete ingredients and mix them to your specification on the spot. All you have to do is transport the concrete and pour it into place. There is no waste as you only pay for the concrete you use. Telephone a local company for details on price and minimum quantity.

Mixing by hand

Use large buckets to measure the ingredients, one for the cement and an identical one for the aggregate, in order to keep the cement perfectly dry. Different shovels are also a good idea. Measure the materials accurately, leveling them with the rim of the bucket. Tap the side of the bucket with the shovel as you load it with sand or cement to shake down the loose particles.

Mix the sand and aggregate first on a hard, flat surface. Scoop a depression in the pile for the measure of cement, and mix all the ingredients until they form an even color.

I Mixing ingredients
Mix the ingredients by chopping the concrete mix with the shovel. Turn the mix over and chop again.

Form another depression and add some water from a watering can. Push the dry ingredients into the water from around the edge until surface water is absorbed, then mix the batch by chopping the concrete with the shovel (**1**). Add more water, turning concrete from the bottom of the pile, and chop it as before until the whole batch has an even consistency. To test the workability of the mix, form a series of ridges by dragging the back of the shovel across the pile (**2**). The surface of the concrete should be flat and even in texture, and the ridges should hold their shape without slumping.

2 Testing the mix
Make ridges with the back of the shovel to test the workability of the mix.

Mixing by machine

Make sure you set up the concrete mixer on a hard, level surface and that the drum is upright before you start the motor. Use a bucket to pour half the measure of coarse aggregate into the drum and add water. This will clean the drum after each batch has been mixed. Add the sand and cement alternately in small batches, plus the rest of the aggregate. Add water little by little along with the other ingredients.

Let the batch mix for a few minutes. Then, with the drum of the mixer still rotating, turn out a little concrete into a wheelbarrow to test its consistency (see above). If necessary, return the concrete to the mixer to adjust it.

MACHINE SAFETY

- Make sure you understand the operating instructions before turning on the machine.
- Prop the mixer level and stable with blocks of wood.
- Never put your hands or shovel into the drum while the mixer is running.
- Don't lean over a rotating drum when you inspect the contents. It is good practice to wear goggles when mixing concrete.

Storing materials

If you buy sand and coarse aggregate in sacks, simply use whatever you need at a time, keeping the rest bagged up until required. If you buy the materials loose, store them in piles, separated by a wooden plank if necessary, on a hard surface or thick polyethylene sheets. Protect the materials from prolonged rain with weighted sheets of plastic.

Storing cement is more critical. It is sold in paper sacks which will absorb moisture from the ground, so pile them on a board propped up on spacers. Keep cement in a dry shed or garage if possible, but if you have to store it outdoors, cover the bags with sheets of plastic weighted down with bricks. Once open, cement can absorb moisture from the air. Keep a partly used bag in a sealed plastic sack.

READY-MIXED CONCRETE

If you need a lot of concrete for a driveway or large patio it may be worth ordering a supply of ready-mixed concrete from a local supplier. Always speak to the supplier well before you need the concrete to discuss your particular requirements. Specify the proportions of the ingredients and say whether you will require the addition of a retarding agent to slow down the setting time. Once a normal mix of concrete is delivered, you will have no more than two hours to finish the job. A retarding agent can add up to two hours to the setting time. Tell the supplier what you need the concrete for and accept his advice.

For quantities of less than 6 cubic yards you might have to shop around for a supplier who is willing to deliver without an additional charge. Discuss any problems of discharging the concrete on site. To avoid transporting the concrete too far by wheelbarrow, have it discharged as close to the site as possible, if not directly into place. The chute on a delivery truck can reach only so far, and if the truck is too large or heavy to drive onto your property you will need several helpers to move the quantity of concrete while it is still workable. A single cubic yard of concrete will fill 25 to 30 large wheelbarrows. If it takes longer than 30 to 40 minutes to discharge the load, you may have to pay extra.

Storing sand and aggregate
Separate the piles of sand and aggregate with a wooden plank.

Storing cement
Raise bags of cement off the ground and cover them with plastic sheeting.

REPAIRING CONCRETE AND STUCCO

Concrete is used in and around the house as a surface for solid floors, drives, paths and walls. In common with other building materials, it suffers from the effects of moisture—spalling and efflorescence—and related defects such as cracking and crumbling. Stucco can also suffer from excessive moisture and may crack as a result of temperature shifts throughout the seasonal cycle. In both cases, if small faults are caught and repaired in time, you may prevent further damage from occurring and stave off costly replacement.

Sealing concrete

New concrete has a high alkali content and efflorescence can develop on the surface as it leaches out. Do not use any finish other than a water-thinned paint until the concrete is completely dry. Treat efflorescence on concrete as for brickwork (▷).

A porous concrete wall should be waterproofed with a clear sealant on the exterior. Some latex paints will cover bitumen satisfactorily, but it will bleed through most paints unless you prime it with a PVA bonding agent diluted 50 percent with water. Alternatively, use an aluminium-based sealer.

Cleaning dirty concrete

Clean dirty concrete as you would brickwork. Where a concrete drive or garage floor, for instance, is stained with patches of oil or grease, soak up fresh spillages immediately to prevent them becoming permanent stains. Sprinkle dry sand onto patches of oil to absorb any liquid deposits, collect it up and wash the area with mineral spirits or degreasing solution.

Binding dusty concrete

Concrete is troweled when it is laid to give a flat finish; if this is overdone, cement is brought to the surface and when the concrete dries out, this thin layer begins to break up within a short time, producing a loose, dusty surface. You must not apply a decorative finish to concrete in this condition.

Treat a concrete wall with stabilizing primer, but paint a dusty floor with one or two coats of PVA bonding agent mixed with five parts of water. Use the same solution to prime a particularly porous surface.

Repairing cracks and holes

Rake out and brush away loose debris from cracks or holes in concrete. If the crack is less than about ¼ inch wide, open it up a little with a cold chisel so that it will accept a filling. Undercut the edges to form a lip so the filler will grip.

To fill a hole in concrete, add a fine aggregate such as gravel to the sand and cement mix. Make sure the fresh concrete sticks in shallow depressions by priming the damaged surface with 3 parts bonding agent: 1 part water. When the primed surface becomes tacky, trowel in the concrete and smooth it. Don't overwork the surface as that will cause improper curing.

Treating spalled concrete

When concrete breaks up or spalls due to the action of frost, the process is accelerated when steel reinforcement is exposed and begins to corrode. Fill the concrete as described above but prepare and prime the metalwork first. If spalling recurs, particularly in exposed conditions, protect the wall with a bitumen base coat and a compatible latex paint.

Spalling concrete ▷
Rusting metalwork causes concrete to spall.

REPAIRING STUCCO

Stucco is a cementious exterior plaster that may be applied directly over block or brick, or over wire lath that has been fastened to wood sheathing. One or two layers of rough stucco are applied, followed by a finish coat.

Large, long cracks in stucco, especially those that run vertically from the roofline and door or window openings, may indicate structural problems that should be remedied before making repairs to the finish. Consult an engineer or builder if you suspect structural faults. Bulges in stucco may mean that the wire lath has pulled loose from the sheathing, a condition that must be corrected before a proper path can be made.

Fine, hairline cracks need no other repair than painting with exterior latex paint. Elastomeric paints are also excellent finishes for stucco because they can expand and contract as the stucco heats and cools without cracking. Rake out larger cracks using a cold chisel, dampen with water and fill flush with the surface with a mortar mix comprised of 1 part portland cement to 4 parts builder's sand and enough water to create a stiff but workable consistency. Use PVA bonding agent to help the patching mixture stick to masonry substrates.

To reinforce especially large cracks or those that seem to open repeatedly, rake out the crack and clean away loose material. Dampen the substrate and crack edges, then fill with mortar mix as described above. Once the patching material has stiffened, apply a coat of bituminous material such as roof cement and embed a piece of fiberglass flashing fabric in it with bitumen and flashing fabric extending at least 3 inches beyond the edges of the crack (1). Flatten and feather the fabric with a roller (2). Wait a day, then apply a second coat of bitumen, and tool or stipple the wet coating to match the texture of the surrounding stucco (3). After it has dried, seal the tar with aluminum primer, then paint.

Large, deep holes in stucco may need to be repaired with two applications of patching mortar. After removing all unsound material and cleaning the area thoroughly, apply a rough coat to the dampened substrate, leaving it about an inch shy of the finished surface. Wait a day or so, then apply the finish coat, working the surface with a hand float to match the surrounding surface texture and feather the edges.

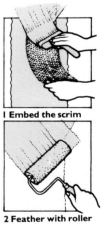

1 Embed the scrim

2 Feather with roller

3 Stipple the texture

MASONRY: CLEANING BRICK AND STONE

At regular intervals and before you decorate the outside of your house, check the condition of the brick and stonework, and carry out any necessary repairs. There's no reason why you can't paint brick or stone walls, but if you consider masonry most attractive in its natural state, you could be faced with a problem: once masonry is painted, it is difficult to restore it to its original condition. There will always be particles of paint left in the texture of brickwork, and even smooth stone, which can be stripped successfully, may be stained by the paint.

Treating new masonry

New brickwork or stonework should be left for about three months until it is completely dry before any further treatment is considered. White, powdery deposits called efflorescence may come to the surface over this period, but you can simply brush it off with a stiff-bristled brush or a piece of burlap. After that, bricks and mortar should be weatherproof and therefore require no further protection or treatment.

Cleaning organic growth from masonry

There are innumerable species of mold growth or lichens, which appear as tiny colored specks or patches on masonry. They gradually merge until the surface is covered with colors ranging from bright orange to yellow or green, gray and black.

Molds and lichen will flourish only in damp conditions, so try to cure the source of the problem before treating the growth (◁). If one side of the house always faces away from the sun, it will have little chance to dry out. Relieve the situation by cutting back overhanging trees or shrubs to increase ventilation to the wall.

Make sure the earth surrounding masonry walls is graded so that surface water flows away from them.

Cracked or corroded downspouts leaking onto the wall are another common cause of organic growth. Feel behind the pipe with your fingers or use a hand mirror to locate the leak.

Removing the growth
Brush the wall vigorously with a stiff-bristled brush. This can be an unpleasant, dusty job, so wear a gauze facemask. Brush away from you to avoid debris being sprayed into your eyes.

Microscopic spores will remain even after brushing. Kill these with a solution of bleach or, if the wall suffers persistently from fungal growth, use a proprietary fungicide, available from most home centers.

Using a bleach solution
Mix one part household bleach with four parts water. Paint the solution onto the wall using an old paintbrush, then 48 hours later wash the surface with clean water, using a scrub brush. Brush on a second application of bleach solution if the original fungal growth was severe.

Using a fungicidal solution
Dilute the fungicide with water according to the manufacturer's instructions and apply it liberally to the wall with an old paintbrush. Leave it for 24 hours, then rinse the wall with clean water. In extreme cases, give the wall two washes of fungicide, allowing 24 hours between applications and a further 24 hours before washing it down with water.

Removing efflorescence from masonry

Soluble salts within building materials such as cement, brick, stone and plaster gradually migrate to the surface along with the water as a wall dries out. The result is a white crystalline deposit called efflorescence.

The same condition can occur on old masonry if it is subjected to more than average moisture. Efflorescence itself is not harmful, but the source of moisture causing it must be identified and cured if the surface is to remain unstained and before painting.

Regularly brush the deposit from the wall with a dry stiff-bristled brush until the crystals cease to form—don't attempt to wash off the crystals; they'll merely dissolve in the water and soak back into the wall. Above all, don't attempt to paint a wall which is still efflorescing, and therefore damp.

When the wall is completely dry, paint the surface with an alkali-resistant primer to neutralize the effect of the crystals before you paint with oil paint; water-thinned paints or clear sealants let the wall breathe, so are not affected by the alkali content of the masonry. Most exterior latex paints can be used without primer (◁).

Stained brickwork

Organic growth

Efflorescence

CLEANING OLD MASONRY

Whether you intend to finish a wall or leave it natural, all loose debris and dirt must be brushed off with a stiff-bristled brush. Don't use a wire brush unless the masonry is badly soiled; the wire brush may leave scratch marks.

Brush along the mortar joints to dislodge loose pointing. Defective mortar can be repaired easily at this stage (see right), but if you fail to disturb it now by being too cautious, it may fall out after you paint, creating far more work in the long run.

Removing unsightly stains

Improve the appearance of stone or brick left in its natural state by washing it with clean water. Play a hose gently onto the masonry while you scrub it with a stiff-bristled brush (1). Scrub heavy deposits with half a cup of ammonia added to a bucketful of water, then rinse again.

Abrade small cement stains or other marks from brickwork with a piece of similar-colored brick, or scrub the area with a household kitchen cleanser.

Remove spilled oil paint from masonry with a proprietary paint stripper. Put on gloves and protective goggles, then paint on the stripper, stippling it into the rough texture (2). After about ten minutes, remove it with a scraper and a soft wire brush. If paint remains in the crevices, dip the brush in stripper and gently scrub it with small circular strokes. When the wall is clean, rinse with water.

1 Remove dirt and dust by washing

2 Stipple paint stripper onto spilled oil paint

REPOINTING MASONRY

The mortar joints between bricks and stones can become porous with age, allowing rainwater to penetrate to the inside, causing damp patches to appear, ruining decorations. Replacing the mortar pointing, which deflects the water, is quite straightforward but time-consuming. Tackle only a small, manageable area at a time, using a ready-mixed mortar or your own mix.

Applying the pointing mortar

Rake out the old mortar pointing with a thin wooden stick to a depth of about ½ inch. Use a cold chisel or a special plugging chisel and sledgehammer to dislodge firmly embedded sections, then brush out the joints with a stiff-bristled brush.

Apply water to the joints using an old paintbrush, making sure the bricks or stones are soaked so they will not absorb too much water from the fresh mortar. Mix up some mortar in a bucket and transfer it to a hawk. If you're mixing your own mortar, use the proportions 1 part cement: 1 part lime: 6 parts builders' sand.

Pick up a little sausage of mortar on the back of a small pointing trowel and push it firmly into the vertical joints. This can be difficult to do without the mortar dropping off, so hold the hawk under each joint to catch it.

Try not to smear the face of the bricks with mortar, as it will stain. Repeat the process for the horizontal joints. The actual shape of the pointing is not vital at this stage.

Once the mortar is firm enough to retain a thumb print, it is ready for shaping. Match the style of pointing used on the rest of the house (see below). When the pointing has almost hardened, brush the wall to remove traces of surplus mortar.

Shaping the mortar joints

The joints shown here are commonly used for brickwork but they are also suitable for stonework. Additionally, stone may have raised mortar joints.

Flush joints
The easiest profile to produce, a flush joint is used where the wall is sheltered or painted. Rub each joint with burlap; start with the verticals.

Rubbed (rounded) joints
Bricklayers make a rubbed or rounded joint with a tool shaped like a sled runner with a handle; the semicircular blade is run along the joints.

Improvise by bending a short length of metal tube or rod. Use the curved section only or you'll gouge the mortar. Alternatively, use a length of ⅜-inch-diameter plastic tube.

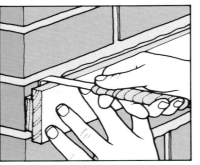

A Frenchman trims weatherstruck joints

Raked joints
A raked joint is used to emphasize the type of bonding pattern of a brick wall. It's not suitable for soft bricks or for a wall that takes a lot of weathering. Scrape out a little of the mortar, then tidy up the joints by running a ⅜-inch stick along them.

Weatherstruck joints
The sloping profile is intended to shed rainwater from the wall. Shape the mortar with the edge of a pointing trowel. Start with the vertical joints, and slope them in either direction but be consistent. During the process, mortar will tend to spill from the bottom of a joint, as surplus is cut off. Bricklayers use a tool called a "frenchman" to neaten the work. It has a narrow blade with the tip bent at right angles. Make your own by bending a thin metal strip, then bind electrical tape around the other end to form a handle. Or bend the tip of an old kitchen knife after heating it with a torch.

You will find it easiest to use a wooden batten to guide the blade of the frenchman along the joints, but nail scraps of plywood at each end of the batten to hold it off the wall.

Align the batten with the bottom of the horizontal joints, then draw the tool along it, cutting off the excess mortar, which drops to the ground.

● **Mortar dyes**
Liquid or powder additives are available for changing the color of mortar to match existing pointing. Color matching is difficult and smears can stain the bricks permanently.

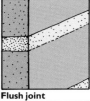

Flush joint

Rubbed joint

Raked joint

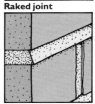

Weatherstruck joint

REPAIRING MASONRY

Cracks in external walls can be either the source of penetrating moisture (◁), which ruins your decoration inside, or the result of a much more serious problem: sinking of the foundations. Whatever the cause, it's obvious that you shouldn't just ignore the danger signs, but effect immediate cures.

Filling cracked masonry

If substantial cracks are apparent in a brick or stone wall, consult a builder or engineer to ascertain the cause.

If the crack seems to be stable, it can be filled. Where the crack follows the line of the mortar joints, rake out those affected and repoint in the normal way, as previously described. A crack that splits one or more bricks or stones cannot be repaired, and the damaged area should be removed and replaced, unless you are going to paint the wall afterwards.

Use a ready-mixed mortar with a little PVA bonding agent added to help it to stick. Soak the cracked masonry with a hose to encourage the mortar to flow deeply into the crack.

Crack may follow pointing only

Cracked bricks could signify serious faults

Priming brickwork

Brickwork will need to be primed only in certain circumstances. An alkali-resistant primer will guard against efflorescence (◁) and a stabilizing solution will bind crumbling masonry and help to seal it at the same time.

If you are planning to paint the wall for the first time with an exterior latex, you may find that the first coat is difficult to apply due to the suction of the dry, porous brick. Thin the first coat slightly with water.

To economize when using a thixotropic latex (◁), prime the wall with a cement paint with a little fine sand mixed in thoroughly.

Waterproofing masonry

Colorless water-repellent fluids are intended to make masonry impervious to water without coloring it or stopping it from breathing (important to allow moisture within the walls to dry out).

Prepare the surface thoroughly before applying the fluid; repair any cracks in bricks or pointing and remove organic growth (◁) and allow the wall to dry out thoroughly.

Apply the fluid generously with a large paintbrush and stipple it into the joints. Apply a second coat as soon as the first has been absorbed to ensure that there are no bare patches where water could seep in. To be sure that you're covering the wall properly, use a sealant containing a fugitive dye, which will disappear gradually after a few weeks.

Carefully paint up to surrounding woodwork; if you accidentally splash sealant onto it, wash it down immediately with a cloth dampened with solvent.

If the area you need to treat is large, consider spraying on the fluid, using a rented spray gun. You'll need to rig up a sturdy work platform and mask off all wood- and metalwork that adjoins the wall. The fumes from the fluid can be dangerous if inhaled, so be sure to wear a proper respirator, which you can also rent.

REPAIRING SPALLED MASONRY

Moisture penetrating soft masonry will expand in icy weather, flaking off the outer face of brickwork and stonework. The process, known as spalling, not only looks unattractive but also allows water to seep into the surface. Repairs to spalled bricks or stones can be made, although the treatment depends on the severity of the problem.

If spalling is localized, it is possible to cut out individual bricks or stones and replace them with matching ones. The sequence below describes how it's tackled with brickwork, but the process is similar for a stone wall.

Spalling bricks caused by frost damage

Where the spalling is extensive, it's likely that the whole wall is porous and your best remedy is to paint on a stabilizing solution to bind the loose material together, then apply a textured wall finish, as used to patch stucco, which will disguise the faults and waterproof the wall at the same time.

Replacing a spalled brick

Use a cold chisel and sledgehammer to rake out the pointing surrounding the brick, then chop out the brick itself. If the brick is difficult to pry out, drill into it many times with a large-diameter masonry bit, then attack the brick with a cold chisel and hammer. It should crumble, enabling you to remove the pieces easily.

To fit the replacement brick, first dampen the opening and spread mortar on the base and one side. Butter the dampened replacement brick on the top and one end and slot it into the hole (1).

Shape the pointing to match the surrounding brickwork then, once it is dry, apply a clear water repellent.

I Replacing a spalled brick
Having mortared top and one end, slip the new brick into the hole you have cut.

PAINTING EXTERIOR MASONRY

The outside walls of your house need painting for two major reasons: to give a clean, bright appearance and to protect the surface from the rigors of the climate. What you use as a finish and how you apply it depend on what the walls are made of, their condition and the degree of protection they need. Bricks are traditionally left bare, but may require a coat of paint if they're in bad condition or previous attempts to decorate have resulted in a poor finish. Stucco walls are often painted to brighten the naturally dull gray color of the cement; sometimes masonry surfaces may need a colorful coat to disguise previous conspicuous patches. On the other hand, you may just want to change the present color of your walls for a fresh appearance.

Working to a plan

Before you start painting the outside walls of your house, plan your time carefully. Depending on the preparation, even a small house will take a few weeks to complete.

You need not tackle the whole job at once, although it is preferable—the weather may change to the detriment of your timetable. You can split the work into separate stages with days (even weeks) in between, so long as you divide the walls into manageable sections. Use window and door frames, bays, pipes and corners of walls to form break lines that will disguise lap marks.

Start at the top of the house, working right to left if you are right-handed (vice versa if you are left-handed).

Concrete floor paints

Floor paints are specially prepared to withstand hard wear. They are especially suitable for concrete garage or workshop floors, but they are also used for stone paving, steps and other concrete structures. They can be used inside for playroom floors.

The floor must be clean and dry and free from oil or grease. If the concrete is freshly laid, allow it to cure for at least three months before painting. Thin the first coat of paint with 10 percent mineral spirits.

Don't use floor paint over a surface sealed with a proprietary concrete sealer, but you can cover other paints so long as they are keyed first.

The best way to paint a large area is to use a paintbrush around the edges, then fit an extension to a paint roller for the bulk of the floor.

SEE ALSO

Details for: ▷
Preparing masonry   28-30

Apply paint with a roller on an extension

	FINISHES FOR MASONRY					
● Black dot denotes compatibility. All surfaces must be clean, sound, dry and free from organic growth.	Cement paint	Exterior latex paint	Reinforced latex paint	Solvent-thinned masonry paint	Textured coating	Floor paint
SUITABLE TO COVER						
Brick	●	●	●	●	●	●
Stone	●	●	●	●	●	●
Concrete	●	●	●	●	●	●
Stucco	●	●	●	●	●	●
Exposed-aggregate concrete	●	●	●	●	●	●
Asbestos cement	●	●	●	●	●	●
Latex paint		●	●	●	●	●
Oil-based paint		●	●	●		●
Cement paint	●	●	●	●	●	●
DRYING TIME: HOURS						
Touch dry	1–2	1–2	2–3	1–2	6	2–3
Recoatable	24	4	24	24	24–48	12–24
THINNERS: SOLVENTS						
Water-thinned	●	●	●		●	
Solvent-thinned				●		●
NUMBER OF COATS						
Normal conditions	2	2	1–2	2	1	1–2
COVERAGE: DEPENDING ON WALL TEXTURE						
Sq. ft. per quart		150–400	120–250	120–225		180–550
Sq. ft. per pound	30–75				20–40	
METHOD OF APPLICATION						
Brush	●	●	●	●	●	●
Roller	●	●	●	●		●
Spray gun	●	●	●	●		●

Paint in manageable sections
You can't hope to paint an entire house in one session, so divide each elevation into manageable sections to disguise the joints. The horizontal molding divide the wall neatly into two sections, and the raised door and window surrounds are convenient break lines.

TECHNIQUES FOR PAINTING MASONRY

SEE ALSO

◁Details for:
Preparing masonry   28-30

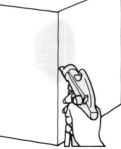

3 Use a banister brush
Tackle deeply textured wall surfaces with a banister brush, using a scrubbing action.

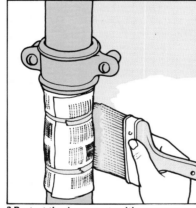

4 Use a roller
For speed in application, use a paint roller with a deep pile for heavy textures, a medium pile for light textures and smooth wall surfaces.

1 Cut in with a gentle scrubbing motion

2 Protect the downspouts with newspaper

5 Spray onto the apex of external corners

6 Spray internal corners as separate surfaces

Using paintbrushes

Choose a 4- to 6-inch-wide paintbrush for walls; larger ones are heavy and tiring to use. A good-quality brush with coarse bristles will last longer on rough walls. For a good coverage, apply the paint with vertical strokes, criss-crossed with horizontal ones. You will find it necessary to stipple paint into textured surfaces.

Cutting in

Painting up to a feature such as a door or window frame is known as cutting in. On a smooth surface, you should be able to paint a reasonably straight edge following the line of the feature, but it's diffiult to apply the paint to a heavily textured wall with a normal brush stroke. Don't just apply more paint to overcome the problem; instead, touch the tip of the brush only to the wall, using a gentle scrubbing action (1), then brush excess paint away from the feature once the texture is filled.

Wipe splashed paint from window and door frames with a cloth dampened with the appropriate thinner.

Painting behind pipes

To protect rainwater downspouts, tape a roll of newspaper around them. Stipple behind the pipe with a brush, then slide the paper tube down the pipe to mask the next section (2).

Painting with a banister brush

Use a banister brush (3) to paint deeply textured masonry surfaces. Pour some paint into a roller tray and dab the brush in to load it. Scrub the paint onto the wall using circular strokes to work it well into the uneven surface.

Using a paint roller

A roller (4) will apply paint three times faster than a brush. Use a deep-pile roller for heavy textures or a medium-pile for lightly textured or smooth walls. Rollers wear quickly on rough walls, so have a spare sleeve handy. Vary the angle of the stroke when using a roller to ensure even coverage and use a brush to cut into angles and obstructions.

A paint tray is difficult to use at the top of a ladder, unless you fit a tool support or, better still, erect a flat platform to work from.

Using a spray gun

Spraying is the quickest and most efficient way to apply paint to a large expanse of wall. But you will have to mask all the parts you do not want to paint, using newspaper and masking tape. The paint must be thinned by about 10 percent for spraying. Set the spray gun according to the manufacturer's instructions to suit the particular paint. It is advisable to wear a respirator when spraying.

Hold the gun about a foot away from the wall and keep it moving with even, parallel passes. Slightly overlap each pass and try to keep the gun pointing directly at the surface—tricky while standing on a ladder. Trigger the gun just before each pass and release it at the end of the stroke.

When spraying a large, blank wall, paint it into vertical bands, overlapping each band about 4 inches.

Spray external corners by aiming the gun directly at the apex so that paint falls evenly on both surfaces (5). When two walls meet at an internal angle, treat each surface separately (6).

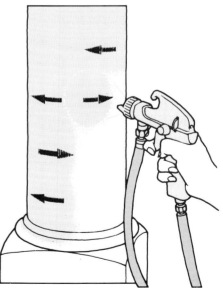

Spray-painting columns
Columns, part of a front door portico, for instance, should be painted in a series of overlapping vertical bands. Apply the bands by running the spray gun from side to side as you work down the column.

ROOFS:PITCHED ROOFS

Most pitched roofs were once built on site from individual lengths of timber, but nowadays, for economy of time and materials, many builders use prefabricated from individual lengths of lumber, but

specifically designed to meet the loading needs of a given house and, unlike traditional roofs, are usually not suitable for conversion because to remove any part of the structure can cause it to collapse.

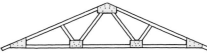

Prefabricated rafter truss

Basic construction

The framework of an ordinary pitched roof is based on a triangle, the most rigid and economical form for a load-bearing structure. The weight of the roof covering is carried by sloping members called rafters, which are set in opposing pairs whose heads meet against a central ridge board running the length of the roof, parallel to the long walls. The lower ends, or feet, of the

rafters, are attached to the top plates of the walls.

To stop the roof's weight from pushing the walls out, horizontal members span between rafter ends. When these are level with the top of the walls they may serve as attic floor joists. In open-ceiling construction they are located nearer the ridge board and are called collar ties.

RIDGE BOARD
RAFTER
COLLAR TIE
ATTIC FLOOR JOIST
WALL PLATE

Parts of a roof

SEE ALSO

Details for: ▷

Roof elements	34
Repairing roof coverings	37-39

PITCHED ROOF TYPES

There are a considerable number of roof styles. Nearly all, however, can be classified among these basic types:

FLAT ROOFS

Flat roofs may be supported on joists to which the ceiling material is also attached, or they may be constructed using trusses which have parallel top and bottom members supported by triangular bracing in between. Most flat roofs actually have a slight slope formed by the roofing material to provide drainage.

SHED OR LEAN-TO ROOFS

This is the simplest type of pitched roof. Sometimes it is called a lean-to roof. Inside the structure, the ceiling may be

attached directly to the rafters, or supported by horizontal joists, forming a sloping loft above.

GABLE ROOFS

Two shed roofs joined together form the classic gable roof, the most commonly used in contemporary construction. Gable roofs are simple and economical to build, and have excellent loadbearing and drainage capabilities. The end (gable) walls are non-loadbearing.

GAMBREL ROOFS

By breaking the slope of a gable roof, more headroom becomes available in the attic area beneath the rafters,

Gambrel and other styles of broken-gable roofs make construction of wide roofs easier also, because it is possible to use shorter lengths of lumber even for spanning large widths.

HIP ROOFS

By sloping the ends of a gable roof toward the center a hip roof is formed. An advantage of this type is the protective overhang formed on all four sides of a house.

INTERSECTING ROOFS

Many houses combine the same or different roof types at angles to each other, to form L- or U-shaped floor plans, as well as other shapes.

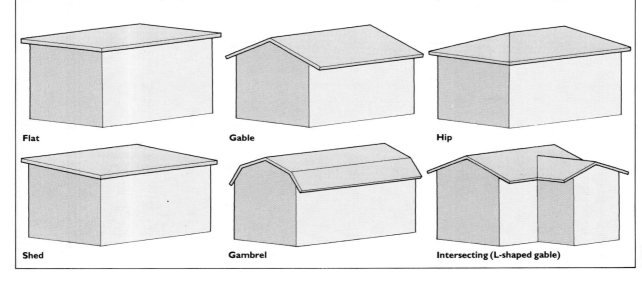

Flat

Gable

Hip

Shed

Gambrel

Intersecting (L-shaped gable)

33

ROOF ELEMENTS

Hips and valleys
Besides the components mentioned earlier, Gable roofs with intersecting dormers or secondary roofs have additional components. This illustration shows the parts and their names.

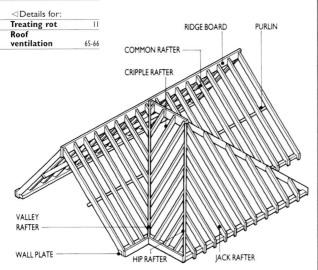

RIDGE BOARD   PURLIN

COMMON RAFTER

CRIPPLE RAFTER

VALLEY RAFTER

WALL PLATE

HIP RAFTER   JACK RAFTER

Hips and valleys

Eaves
The overhang of rafters past the outer walls is called the eaves, but sometimes rafters are cut flush with the walls and a fascia board along their ends protects them and supports the guttering (1). Projecting rafters can be left open, the ends exposed (2), and gutter brackets screwed to their sides or top edge.

1 Flush eaves

Closed eaves
The back of a fascia is usually grooved to take a soffit board, which closes the eaves (3). The board can be at 90 degrees to the wall or slope with the rafters, and it can be of various weatherproof materials. If attic insulation is laid, a roof with closed eaves must be ventilated by a small gap between soffit board and wall or by fitted vents (◁).

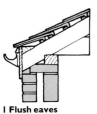

2 Open eaves

The rake
The rake is the sloping edge of the roofing and can end flush with the wall or project past it. A flush rake means a roof structure that stops at the wall, with end rafters placed close to it and the roofing overlying it (4). An overhanging rake means framing extending beyond the wall to carry a fly rafter and fascia with a fascia fixed to it. Behind the fascia may be a soffit board to conceal the fly rafter (5).

3 Closed eaves

ROOF STRUCTURE PROBLEMS

A roof structure can fail when members decay through inadequate weatherproofing, condensation or insect attack. It can also result from overloading caused by too-light original members, a new roof covering of heavier material or the cutting of a window opening that is not properly braced. You can detect any movement of a roof structure from outside. From ground level any sagging of the roof will be seen in the lines of the roof covering.

INSPECTION

The roof should also be inspected from inside. In any case, this should be done annually to check the weathering and for freedom from pest infestation. Work in a good light. If your attic has no lighting use a "trouble light" plugged into a downstairs wall socket. In an unfloored attic place boards across the joists.

ROT AND INFESTATION

Rot in roof timbers is a serious problem which should be corrected by experts, but its cause should also be identified and promptly dealt with (◁).

Rot is caused by damp conditions that encourage wood-rotting fungi to grow. Inspect the roof covering closely for loose or damaged elements in the general area of the rot, although on a pitched roof water may be penetrating the covering at a higher level and so not be immediately obvious. If the rot is close to a gable wall you should suspect the flashing. Rot can also be caused by condensation, the remedy for which is usually better ventilation.

If you bring in contractors to treat the rot it is better to have them make all the repairs. Their work is covered by a guarantee which may be invalidated if you attempt to deal with the cause yourself to save money.

Insect infestation should also be dealt with by professionals if it is serious. Severely affected wood may have to be cut out and replaced, and the whole structure will have to be fumigated to ensure the problem is remedied.

STRENGTHENING THE ROOF

A roof that shows signs of sagging may have to be braced, though it may not be necessary if a sound structure has stabilized and the roof is weatherproof. In some old buildings a slightly sagging roof line is considered attractive.

Consult an engineer if you suspect a roof is weak. Apart from a sagging roof line, the walls under the eaves should be inspected for bulging and checked with a plumb line. Bulging may occur where window openings are close to the eaves, making a wall relatively weak. It may be due to the roof spreading because of inadequate fastening of the ties and rafters. If this is the case, call in a builder or roofing contractor to make the necessary alterations and improvements.

A lightly constructed roof can be made stronger by adding extra structural members. The method chosen will depend on the type of roof, its span, its loading and its condition. Where the lengths or section of new members are not too large the repair may be possible from inside. If not, at least some of the roof covering may have to be stripped off. Any given roof must be assessed and the most economical solution found for the particular circumstances.

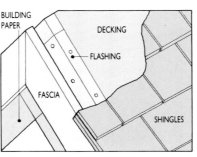

BUILDING PAPER

DECKING

FLASHING

FASCIA

SHINGLES

4 Flush rake

RAFTER

JOIST

RIDGEBOARD
GABLE PLATE
LADDER
SOFFIT
FASCIA
PLATE
FLY RAFTER

5 Overhanging rake

ROOF COVERINGS

Generally speaking, the more durable the roof covering, the more expensive it will be, both in materials and labor costs. Try to afford a roof covering with an expected durability of at least 20 years. Besides cost, making a wise roof-covering decision must take into consideration structural factors (heavy roofs such as slate and tile often require more-than-ordinary roof framing), fire-resistance and appearance.

Types

Asphalt shingles: This is the most common roof covering used in the United States. Inexpensive, easy to install and repair, relatively durable, and providing tight protection from wind and rain, asphalt shingles come in many colors, textures and patterns. Different weights have different life-spans. Shingles weighing 235 pounds or more per "square" (the amount needed to cover 100 square feet) normally last 15 to 25 years. Though asphalt shingles are by far the most common type of roof covering, there are many other options.

Roll roofing: This is made from the same material as asphalt shingles, but is manufactured in long rolls. Roll roofing is applied in overlapping layers, giving it a varying lifespan of from 5 to 20 years depending upon the amount of overlap. Roll roofing is inexpensive, easy and quick to apply, but lacks good appearance. Do-it-yourself homebuilders often consider applying a roll roof initially, then reroofing with higher-quality material later when financing permits. Roll-roofing is only partially fire-resistant.

Wood shingles: These are normally sawn from cedar or redwood, come in uniform lengths and thicknesses, and when applied lie flat and smooth on the roof. Two grades are used: one for the starter course and the other for the rest of the roof. A separate grade is used for walls. Wood shingles add beauty and resale value to a home. However, though easy to install, the process is time-consuming, and the shingles themselves are expensive. Wood shingles offer no fire-resistance unless treated and are prohibited in some areas.

Wood shakes: Wood shakes are normally split from logs, rather than sawn, making them somewhat thicker and more irregularly-shaped than shingles. Resawn shakes—split shakes sawn in half through their thickness—have one smooth side and one rough, so they lie flatter when installed. Shakes may last 40 years or more, and because of their looks and durability add very high resale value to a home. Shakes frequently cost twice as much as asphalt shingles, and take much longer to apply. Like wood shingles, they are combustible.

Metal: Very expensive terne and copper roofing is available, but most homeowners choosing metal roof-covering select galvanized steel sheet or aluminum, which comes in 2-foot-wide strips up to 18 feet long. The panels overlap each other along raised crimps through which they are nailed with special nails. Sheet-metal roofing is very easy to apply, and has a life-span of 30 to 60 years. Sheet-metal roofing is also inexpensive, costing about the same as asphalt shingles yet requiring less labor to install. Metal roofs do not add appreciable resale value, however.

Slate: Because of its high expense and difficulty of application, slate is seldom used for new roofs, especially in areas where slate is not naturally-occurring. However, slate roofs frequently outlast their houses, and add high resale value. Slates are easily broken by falling tree branches, and their dark color retains heat in summer. Slate is, of course, fireproof.

Tile: There are several types on the market. Traditional clay tiles are time-consuming and difficult to apply; newer concrete tiles are easier and quicker, and some do not require extensive roof framing. Tile is beautiful, durable (30- to 60-year lifespan), and fireproof. But materials and labor expense is high and like slate, tile breaks easily under impact.

SEE ALSO

Details for: ▷
Repairing roof coverings 37-39
Roll roofing 41

Asphalt shingles

Roll roofing

Wood shingles

Wood shakes

Slate

Tile

SLOPE AND PITCH

Slope and pitch are often incorrectly used as synonyms. While both terms do refer to the incline of a roof, slope identifies the incline as a ratio of the roof's vertical rise to the horizontal run of one side, but pitch identifies the incline as a ratio of the rise to *twice* the run, thus taking into account both sides of the roof.

Sometimes slope is expressed as a fraction, but, to use as an example a roof that rises 4 inches for each foot (12 inches) of run, usually such an incline is referred to as having a "4-in-12 slope." Pitch, on the other hand, is always expressed as a fraction. The pitch of a roof with a 4-in-12 slope is 1/6.

SLOPE = RISE / RUN   PITCH = RISE / 2 × RUN

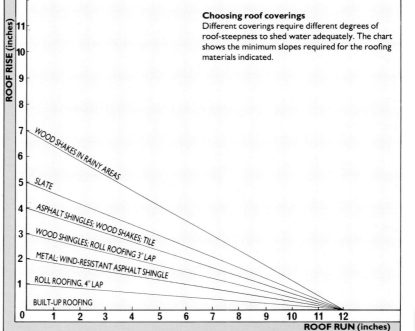

Choosing roof coverings
Different coverings require different degrees of roof-steepness to shed water adequately. The chart shows the minimum slopes required for the roofing materials indicated.

ROOF RISE (inches)

WOOD SHAKES IN RAINY AREAS
SLATE
ASPHALT SHINGLES; WOOD SHAKES; TILE
WOOD SHINGLES; ROLL ROOFING 3" LAP
METAL; WIND-RESISTANT ASPHALT SHINGLE
ROLL ROOFING, 4" LAP
BUILT-UP ROOFING

ROOF RUN (inches)

CHECKING FOR LEAKS

Most roof leaks become noticeable when they produce wet spots on ceilings.

Seldom, though, are the sources for leaks directly above the spots.

Analyzing the symptoms

Leaks near where chimneys pass close to walls or through roofs are relatively easy to pinpoint: generally they are the result of defective or damaged flashing. Leaks which appear elsewhere indicate the need for roof repair.

If the house has an unfinished attic, simply examine the underside of the decking near the wet spot during a rainstorm. Use a strong light, preferably a "trouble light" equipped with a 100-watt bulb. If the leak is not visible over the spot, search "uphill" of the leak until you find droplets of water entering through the decking at some point. You should then be able to trace their trail down to the spot. You can make a temporary repair by applying caulking compound over the area where the water is entering. Be sure to press the sealer in tightly. Or, you may opt for the traditional remedy of placing a large pan beneath a dripping area and emptying it as it becomes full. In either case, you should make permanent repairs as soon as possible. On the day of the repair, start by driving a small nail through the roof from the underside so that you can locate the leak from outside on the roof surface.

If the underside of the roof decking is covered, you may still be able to estimate the leak's source from below, and remove batts of insulation until you locate the trouble spot. However, if the attic is finished with wallboard, your only course of action is to locate the leak from the outside.

To do this, measure from the wet spot on the ceiling to some point of reference that is also visible outside, such as the chimney. Then, go up on the roof and duplicate the measurement. Search around the point and above it, bearing in mind that water can travel horizontally and diagonally in addition to straight down from its source to the point of entry, but it can never travel uphill. Look for curled, cracked or missing shingles, torn roofing paper, rotted decking, corroded flashing, any place that suggests it might admit moisture, especially if driven by wind.

Be especially cautious when climbing around on roofs. Wear sneakers and clothing that allows unrestricted movement, and stay off roofs in wet or very windy weather. Also, don't walk on roofing materials in near—or below—freezing temperatures, or in extremely hot weather. Cold makes asphalt brittle; heat can cause it to stretch and tear. In either situation you risk doing more damage to the roof than has already occurred. Under such conditions, or if the roof is steep-sloped or is covered with naturally-fragile materials (slate, tile, asbestos-cement shingles) use a lightweight roof ladder that hooks over the peak of the roof and affords safe access while distributing weight over a broad area.

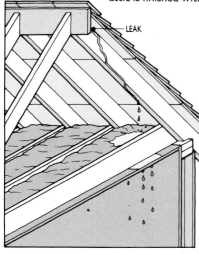

Locate leaks from inside

LEAK

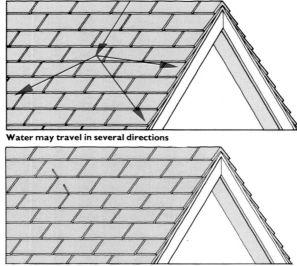

Water may travel in several directions

Drive nails to find leaks from outside

HANDLING LADDERS

When using a ladder, always be sure it is well-seated at the base, and that it extends at least 2 to 3 feet above the highest point you will be working on, so that you will have something to hold onto especially if you will be climbing on and off the ladder to reach the roof. Have a helper support the ladder from below while you are climbing up or down.

Carrying a ladder
Hold the ladder nearly vertical, braced with your body. Keep the base close to the ground.

Locating a ladder
Locate the foot of a ladder away from the wall ¼ the distance of its height; an angle of about 75°.

Working from a ladder
Do not reach sideways beyond the point where you must move your hips past the rails.

ROOF SAFETY

Working on a roof can be hazardous, and if you are unsure of yourself on heights you should call in a contractor to do the work. If you do decide to do it yourself, do not use ladders alone for roof work. Rent a sectional scaffold tower and scaffold boards to provide a safe working platform.

Roof coverings are fairly fragile and should not be walked on. Rent crawl boards or special roof ladders to gain access. A roof ladder should reach from the scaffold tower to the roof's ridge and hook over it. On some models wheel the ladder up the slope and then turn it over to engage the hook (1).

Roof ladders are made with rails that keep the treads clear of the roof surface and spread the load (2), but if you think it's necessary you can place additional padding of paper-stuffed or sand-filled sacks to help spread the load further.

Never leave tools on the roof when they are not being used, and keep those that are needed safely contained inside the ladder framework.

1 Engage the hook of the ladder over the ridge

2 Roof ladders spread the load

REPAIRING ROOF COVERINGS

Repairing asphalt shingles

Curled shingles or those slightly torn or broken off can be repaired. Badly damaged shingles should be replaced. It is best to take the weather into account:

Work on a warm, sunny day if possible, so that shingle material will be pliable but not soft to the touch. Cold stiffens shingles, causing them to crack easily.

1 Fixing lifted or curled shingles
Apply a spot of roofing cement to the underside, then weight shingle with a brick. For torn shingles, apply cement liberally, press shingle down and nail both edges. Apply caulk, silicone sealer or roofing cement to nail holes before nailing heads down.

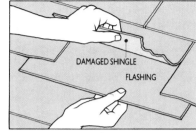

2 Repairing broken shingles
Cut a piece of metal flashing to size of original plus 3 in. on all sides. Apply roofing cement to underside of flashing, slide it in place beneath damaged shingle, then apply cement to top of flashing and press damaged shingle onto to it.

Replacing a shingle

1 Replacing a shingle
Remove it from beneath those above. Carefully lift them and pry out the nails underneath using a putty knife and pry bar. If they won't come out, hammer them flat by laying the pry bar on the heads and striking it with hammer.

2 Sliding the new shingle into place
Align bottom edge of new shingle with the edges of the shingles on either side. Nail it in place, starting at one side and nailing across. Be sure overlapping shingles cover the nails by at least 1 in. Apply cement to the shingles lifted, and weight them flat.

Hips and ridges

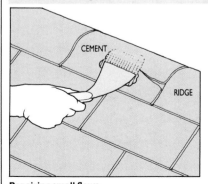

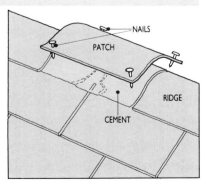

Repairing small flaws
Cover small damaged areas with roofing cement. If damage is more extensive, repair with flashing as shown above or with a patch made of shingle (shown here). Apply cement to the damaged shingle, press the patch over it and nail all four corners. Apply caulk, silicone sealer or roofing cement to nail holes before nailing heads down to discourage leaking.

SEE ALSO

Details for: ▷

Reroofing	42-43
Flashing	44-45

REPAIRING ROOF COVERINGS

Repairing wood shingles

Thorough ventilation is the key to preserving wood shingles. Unless they can dry out after becoming wet they will rot. Shingle roofs often have wide spaces between decking boards to allow significant air flow underneath. However, even if solid decking such as plywood is used, underlayment—usually asphalt-saturated felt paper—is omitted between decking and shingles,

and between courses of shingles themselves. Under- and interlayment is recommended under and between wood shakes.

Work from a roof ladder when repairing wood shingles, to avoid damaging brittle shingles. The best time for shingle repair is the day after a soaking rain, when the shingles are still soft.

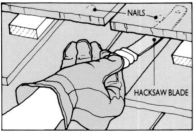

I Using wedges
Drive wedges beneath damaged shingle and overlapping shingles in upper course.

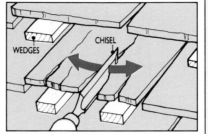

2 Removing damaged shingle
Remove damaged shingle by splitting it apart using a chisel.

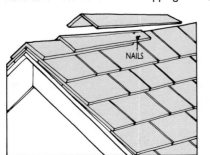

3 Sawing through nails
Saw through nails holding damaged shingle. Use a hacksaw blade wrapped with duct tape.

4 Installing new shingle in line with others
Leave ¼-in. gap on each side. Nail in place 1 in. from edges and top.

Replacing hips and ridges

Where shingles meet at hip and ridge seams, the most common treatment is the Boston ridge, which is formed by nailing together pairs of shingles or 1-inch-thick (nominal) boards along the seam. Nails holding each pair to the roof are covered by the overlapping pair next to it. Alternate the overlapping

ends of the boards making up each pair. As an alternative, several pairs of long boards can be butt-joined. To splice the boards, apply a layer of caulk to the ends and portions of the top and bottom surfaces, then nail metal flashing across the seam, pressing it down into the caulk.

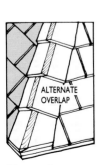

Hip covering

Boston ridge

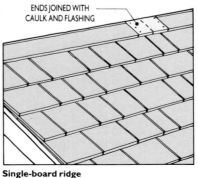

Single-board ridge

REPLACING A TILE

Individual tiles can be difficult to remove for two reasons: the retaining nibs on their back edges and their interlocking shape which holds them together.

You can remove a broken plain tile by simply lifting it so that the nibs clear the batten on which they rest, then drawing it out. This is made easier if the overlapping tiles are first lifted with wooden wedges inserted at both sides of the tile to be removed (I).

If the tile is also nailed try rocking it loose. If this fails you will have to break it out carefully. You may then have to use a slate hook or hacksaw blade to extract or cut any remaining nails.

Use a similar technique for single-lap interlocking tiles, but in this case you will also have to wedge up the tile to the left of the one being removed (2). If the tile is of a deep profile you will have to ease up a number of the surrounding tiles to get the required clearance.

If you are taking out a tile to put in a roof ventilator unit you can afford to smash it with a hammer. But take care not to damage any of the adjacent tiles. The remaining tiles should be easier to remove once the first is out.

I Lift the overlapping tiles with wedges

2 Lift interlocking tiles above and to the left

CUTTING TILES

To cut tiles use an abrasive cutting disc in a power saw or rent an angle grinder for the purpose. Always wear protective goggles and a mask when cutting with a power tool.

For small work use a tungsten grit blade in a hacksaw frame or, if trimming only, use pincers but score the cutting line first with a tile cutter.

REBEDDING RIDGE TILES

Ridge tiles on old roofs often become loose because of a breakdown of the old lime mortar.

To rebed ridge tiles, first lift them off and clear all the old crumbling mortar from the roof, and from the undersides of the tiles.

Give the tiles a good soaking in water before starting to fasten them. Mix a new bedding mortar of 1 part cement to 3 parts sand. It should be a stiff mix and not at all runny. Load about half a bucketful and carry it on to the roof.

Dampen the top courses of the roof tiles and apply the mortar with the trowel to form a continuous edge bedding about 2 inches wide and 3 inches high, following the line left behind by the old mortar.

Where the ridge tiles butt together, or come against a wall, place a solid bedding of mortar, inserting pieces of tile in it to reduce shrinkage. Place the mortar for all the tiles in turn, setting each tile into place and pressing it firmly into the mortar. Strike off any squeezed-out mortar cleanly with the trowel, without smearing the tile. Ridge tiles should not be pointed.

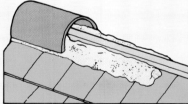
Apply bands of bedding mortar on each side

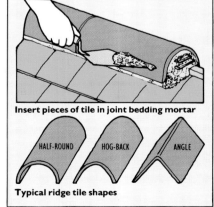
Insert pieces of tile in joint bedding mortar

HALF-ROUND   HOG-BACK   ANGLE

Typical ridge tile shapes

REPAIRING ROOF COVERINGS

Mending metal roofing

Leaks due to broken nail heads, splits and small punctures can be patched with flashing cement or fiberglass asphalt-patching cement sold by building suppliers. If new roof sections are needed, try to match the old ones. Obtain sections long enough to reach from ridge to eaves if possible. Otherwise, overlap seams at least 6 inches and be sure top sections overlap those underneath. Lap vertical seams away from direction of prevailing winds. New galvanized roofing will not hold paint until weathered, usually one year. Wear sneakers when working on metal roofs; also gloves, especially if metal is hot.

SEE ALSO

Details for: ▷
Reroofing   42-43
Flashing   44-45

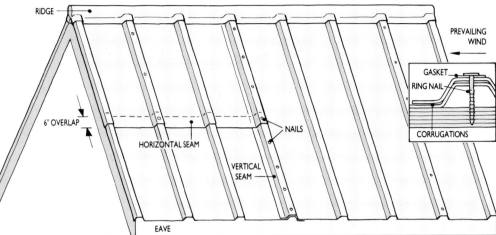

Installing new roof section
To install new roof section, overlap corrugations. Nail through ridges into decking. Use neoprene-gasketed ring-shank nails to prevent leaks and to hold fast despite fluctuations of metal due to temperature changes.

Removing and replacing a slate

A slate may slip out of place because its nails become corroded or because of a breakdown of the material of the slate itself. Whatever the cause, slipped or broken slates must be replaced as soon as possible.

Use a slate hook to remove the trapped part of a broken slate. Slip the tool under the slate and locate its hooked end over one of the nails (**1**), then pull down hard on the tool to extract or cut through the nail. Remove the second nail in the same way. Even where an aged slate has already slipped out completely you may have to remove the nails in the same way to allow the replacement slate to be slipped in.

You will not be able to nail the new slate in place. Instead cut a 1-inch-wide strip of copper to the length of the slate lap plus 1 inch and nail the strip to the sheathing, securing it between the slates of the lower course (**2**). Then slide the new slate into position and turn back the end of the lead strip to secure it (**3**).

Cutting slate

With a sharp point mark out the right size on the back of the slate, either by measuring it out or scribing around another slate of that size. Place the slate, bevelled side down, on a bench, the cutting line level with the bench's edge, then chop the slate with the edge of a bricklayer's trowel. Work from both edges towards the middle, using the edge of the bench as a guide. Mark the nail holes and punch them out with a nail or drill them with a bit the size of the nails. Support the slate well while making the holes.

Asbestos cement slates
These can be cut by scribing the lines, then breaking the slates over a straight edge or sawing with a general-purpose saw. If you saw them, wear a mask, keep dust damped down well and sweep it into a plastic bag for disposal.

1 Pull out nails

2 Nail strip to sheathing

3 Fold strip over edge

Cut from each edge

FLAT AND ROLL ROOFING

Flat (built-up) roofs

Flat roofs (most of which actually have a very slight pitch to promote drainage) depend on a seamless waterproof membrane to prevent leaks. Although some flat roofs are made of metal, the most common are made up of alternating layers of asphalt-saturated roofing felt and either liquid asphalt or melted coal tar. The first layer is nailed to the roof dry (with no liquid underneath) to prevent subsequent coatings from leaking through to the ceiling. Gravel, crushed stone or marble chips are spread over the top surface to reflect heat (which preserves the roofing) and provide coloring. Substitutes for the liquid coating—which must be applied hot—have recently come on the market and include synthetic rubber, mastic, fiberglass, and other compounds, all of which may be applied cold but with varying results. Unless only minor repairs are present, it is usually best to have flat roofs resurfaced professionally.

Roll roofing

Roll roofing can be used on both flat and pitched roofs. It is sold in 36-foot rolls, 3 feet wide, and is applied using wide-head galvanized or aluminum shingle nails. On flat roofs and those with slopes to 1-in-12, each course is laid so that it overlaps the one underneath it by 19 inches. This method is called "double-coverage." Roll roofing designed to be applied in this way is made with only about half the width of the material coated with mineral granules. The smooth portion, which lies underneath each overlapping course, is called the selvage. On steeper roofs with slopes to 3-in-12, roll roofing with only 4-inch-wide, and even 3-inch-wide, selvage may be used. Because so little of each course overlaps the one beneath it this method of application is called "single-coverage." Roll roofing is easy to apply, repair and reapply. However, it must be unrolled in place the day before installation to allow it to expand, soften, and lie flat; otherwise it will buckle. When nailing roll roofing, always work from one end of a strip to the other, never from the ends toward the middle.

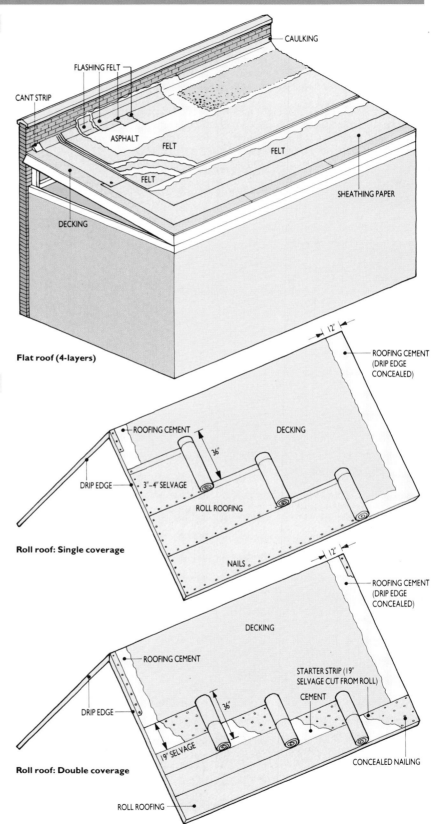

Flat roof (4-layers)

Roll roof: Single coverage

Roll roof: Double coverage

REPAIRING FLAT ROOFS

Mending blisters and splits

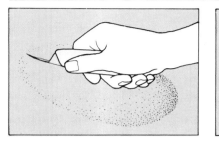

1 Slice through blistered layers
Use a sharp utility knife, and leave lower layers of roofing intact.

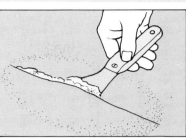

2 Work roofing cement under loose felt
Apply cement under both sides of slit, using a flexible-blade putty knife.

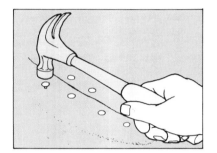

3 Nail both sides of split flat
Use wide-headed galvanized or aluminum shingle nails on both sides of the cut.

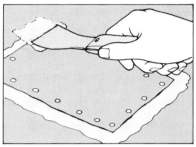

4 Cover repair with roof cement
Add patch of shingle. Nail patch around edges; seal with cement.

Patching damaged areas

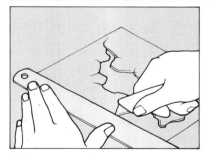

1 Cut out damaged area
Use sharp utility knife. Use straightedge to make square or rectangular cut.

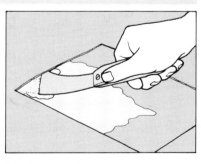

2 Apply roofing cement to exposed area
Using putty knife, lift edges carefully and force cement underneath as well.

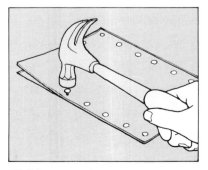

3 Nail down exact-size patch of shingle
Layer several together if necessary to bring patch level with the finished surface.

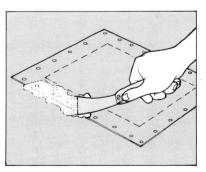

4 Apply cement, then nail down top patch
Top patch should be cut 2 in. oversize. Seal edges and nails with cement.

INSPECTION

Inspect flat roofs once a year. Do the job in two stages: once on a dry day, and again just after a rain so that you can observe standing pools of water. Wear soft-soled shoes and walk gently; one of the chief causes of leaks in a built-up roof is breakdown caused by careless walking on the roof in heavy work boots. If the roof is visited frequently install a wooden walkway supported on 2×4s laid horizontally to spread weight and distribute pressure over a large area. This prevents damage.

Leaks are generally located directly over their evidence on the ceiling below. Chief causes of leaks are moisture trapped between layers of roofing due to incorrect application, drying out or cracking of the layers due to deterioration caused by ultraviolet radiation, and inadequate flashing of roof edges and openings. Most leaks, in fact, appear where the roof meets the edges of the building.

Clean away debris—especially areas of damp slit or debris—from the roof and gutters. Look for blisters or ripples in the roof surface, as well as slits, cracks, areas of torn roofing and places where flashing has come loose or deteriorated. Do not tamper with untorn blisters or loose flashing until you are ready to make repairs. Blisters not located near ceiling damage and which do not expel water when pressure is applied should not be disturbed or repaired.

Treating the whole surface

A roof which has already been patched and is showing general signs of wear and tear can be given an extra lease on life by covering it with black asphalt roof coating—not roofing cement—especially designed for the purpose. Coating is available at many building supply and hardware stores.

First sweep the roof thoroughly to remove any loose debris, including pebbles which may have been part of the original roof covering. Then, apply the coating with a long-handled brush made for the job. Work only a small area at a time, resweeping as you go. Be sure to start at the highest point on the roof and work downward, also leaving yourself an escape route. Cover this path later, after the rest of the roof has dried. Spreading gravel or stone chips over modern flat-roof coatings is usually unnecessary. Consult the supplier or manufacturer to be sure.

SEE ALSO

Details for: ▷

Flashing repairs	45

REROOFING PITCHED ROOFS

When roofing has become so worn that massive or frequent repairs are needed, it is often more feasible to renew the entire roof. However, before you order the work, inspect the decking and rafters for signs of rot or damage. If the roof is quite old or you suspect it is unsound, perform the inspection first from in the attic underneath, to avoid risking an accident by walking on weakened roof members. Probe exposed wood with a penknife or awl. Remove insulation batts if necessary. Look for spongy or crumbly wood—indicating rot—and stained areas which mark present or past areas of leakage. Rotten areas must be replaced. If extensive, the entire roof should be resheathed and perhaps reframed.

New roofing over old

New asphalt or wood shingles can usually be laid directly over a single layer of old shingles, provided the roof deck and framing underneath is sound and the original shingles are not badly warped. New shingles, unless they are wood laid over an old layer of asphalt, will in time mold to the shape of those underneath, exaggerating any irregularities. Roofs with slopes greater than 6-in-12 may accept three layers of shingles provided the rafters are at least 2×8 and the combined weight of the additional shingles plus load factors meets code requirements. Check with your building inspector when planning the job.

To prepare an ordinary asphalt-shingled roof for reroofing, renail all loose or warped shingles and patch broken ones with asphalt scraps nailed in place to fill out their contours.

Remove any protruding nails. Break back shingles along the borders of the roof so they lie flush with the edges (or break them back further and attach lengths of 1×6 lumber as nailing surfaces) and install metal drip-edge flashing around the edge of the roof. Remove the ridge shingles.

Apply new shingles as you would to felt underlayment. Remove the nails from chimney and pipe flashing as you reach them and slide the new shingles underneath. When renailing flashing, apply roofing cement as well. At TV antennas, remove each guy wire as you reach it then refasten it in a new spot—and dab roofing cement over the fitting—after shingling the area. Around the mast plate, cut new shingles carefully and cover the seams with roofing cement.

Pry bar

Ice chopper

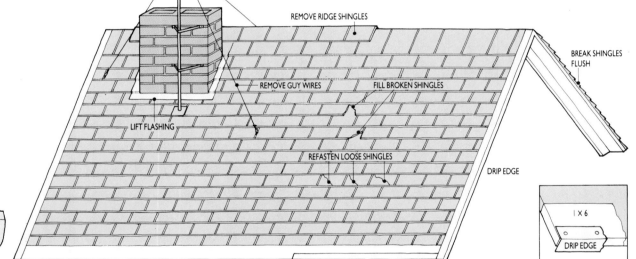

REMOVE RIDGE SHINGLES

BREAK SHINGLES FLUSH

REMOVE GUY WIRES

FILL BROKEN SHINGLES

LIFT FLASHING

REFASTEN LOOSE SHINGLES

DRIP EDGE

1 × 6

DRIP EDGE

Stripping shingles

Badly warped roofs or those with several layers of shingles must be stripped before reroofing. Popular tools for this job are a long-handled ice chopper and a short, flat steel pry bar.

Choose a period of fair weather for working, and strip only as large an area as you can cover securely in case of rain. Work from a ladder or scaffold to remove the lower shingle courses then attach roofing jacks to the decking to remove shingles farther up. Spread plastic or a tarp on the ground below to make clean up easier. Bare roof decks can be slippery, so wear non-slip shoes and use extreme caution.

Roofing jacks

Roofing jacks, available at rent-it centers or easily made on the job, are wood or steel triangular brackets used for supporting horizontal planks along the length of pitched roofs. They're essential for safety when working on steeply pitched roofs. The brackets fasten with nails directly into the roof deck. The nail holes are filled with roof cement on removal. Commercial jacks adjust to match the slope of the roof.

Use 3 jacks to support a 16-foot length of 2×10 plank (or 2 brackets per 8-foot span). Install the end jacks first, using at least three 8d nails per bracket, then the middle one(s).

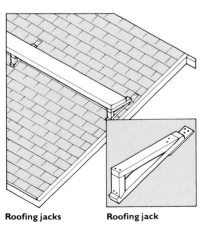

Roofing jacks   **Roofing jack**

REROOFING PITCHED ROOFS

Underlayment

Except with wood shingles, where optimum ventilation is essential, new decking and decking stripped of old roofing should be covered with 15-pound asphalt-saturated felt paper as underlayment. Felt paper prevents the passage of moisture but not vapor. Do not use plastic sheeting.

Professional roofers often cover the entire roof with underlayment before reshingling because of the extra protection it affords the deck in case of rain. However, because wind easily damages thin felt paper, you may wish to apply underlayment in stages.

To apply underlayment, first be sure the decking surface is dry, smooth, and free of protruding nails and splinters. Apply roofing cement to the upper surface of the drip edge and along the seam where it meets the decking, then set the roll of paper at one end of the roof and unroll it horizontally, allowing ¼ inch of the drip edge to extend beyond the paper. Staple the paper to the decking in as few places as possible, just enough to hold it in place until new shingles can be applied over top. Overlap subsequent courses of paper 2 inches over the course below; 4 inches at vertical seams. Always staple from one end of the course to the other to avoid producing a ripple in the center. At roof or hip ridges, fold the paper over the peak from each side to produce a double thickness. At valleys, overlap the flashing 4 inches on each side, also producing a double thickness of paper. Fasten the underlayment to the flashing using wide-head roofing nails made of metal compatible with the flashing material.

Bevel strips

When reroofing over wood or multi-layer asphalt shingles, the new layer of shingles will severely distort unless the tops of the new shingles are placed gainst the bottoms (butts) of the old. To level the old roof surface and permit greater freedom in laying the new shingles, nail strips of beveled wood siding against the butts of shingles before applying the new layer. Strips also form a solid nailing base for new shingles. Rip the siding so that its thickest edge equals the thickness of the shingle butts and attach it with that edge adjacent to the old shingles. Use 8d nails driven into rafters beneath decking.

Applying 3-tab asphalt shingles

Begin shingling at the eaves. First attach a single course of full-length shingles (trim 3 inches from their width at the tab ends) top-edge down along the length of the roof using wide-head shingle nails. Extend the shingles ¼-inch beyond the drip edge. Then nail a second layer of full-size shingles top-edge up over the first layer to complete the starter course.

So that the cutouts in each shingle will always center over the tabs in the course below, remove half a tab from the first shingle starting the second course. Attach the shingle so it exposes 6 inches of the one beneath. Lay the rest of the course, nailing 1 inch and 12 inches from each end, ⅝ inch above the cutouts. Space subsequent shingles to provide the same exposure. After completing the second course, start the third, removing an entire tab from the first shingle in the course.

Snap a horizontal chalk line measured from the eaves to mark the upper edge of the fourth course. Use a shingle with 1½ tabs removed to start, then lay the shingles to the line to compensate for errors in the previous 3 courses. Repeat the entire 4-stage process until you reach the ridge, then work up from the other side of the roof. Trim shingles to lie along the ridge. Cover their top edges with a strip of flashing folded lengthwise, then apply overlapping single shingle-tabs. Cover the nail heads of the last shingle with roofing cement to prevent leakage.

SEE ALSO

Details for:▷
Roof coverings   35

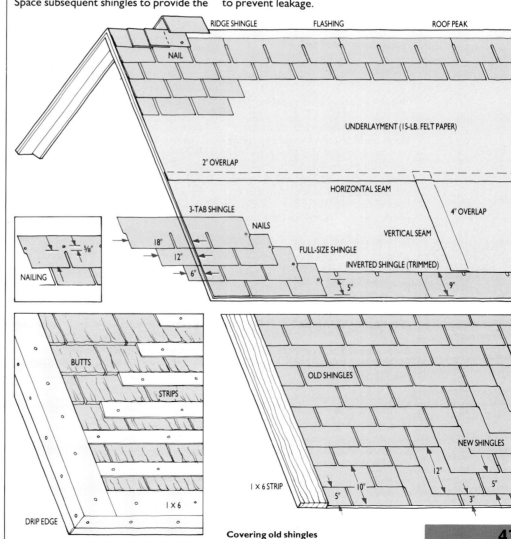

Details for reroofing over wood shingles

Covering old shingles
Trim and apply new shingles against butts of old layer.

43

FLASHING

Flashing is used to prevent moisture from entering under the roof covering wherever two or more planes of a roof meet or wherever the roof meets a vertical surface. It is also used along edges of roofs and other windows and doorways to direct moisture away from the house exterior and

structural framing. Roll roofing material is widely used for flashing, particularly along ridges and hips, and at valleys. However, the most durable flashing materials are sheet aluminum, copper or galvanized steel. All are sold in rolls especially for the purpose.

SEE ALSO
◁Details for:
Checking for leaks   36

Inspecting flashing

Inspect flashing at least once a year. It is a prime location for roof leaks. Look for cracks and separations where the flashing meets the chimney, vent stack, dormer and abuttment walls, and where

roof planes meet at valleys. Sometimes damaged flashing is discolored. Very old flashing sometimes develops pinholes which are hard to see so if possible, check the roof from below for leaks.

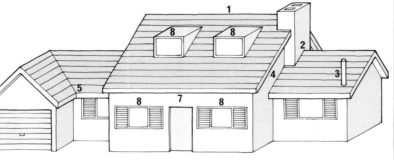

**Flashing locations
(typical)**
1 Ridge
2 Chimney
3 Vent stack
4 Vertical wall
5 Valley
6 Rake
7 Eave
8 Drip edge

Maintenance and repair

It is not a bad idea to coat all flashing seams periodically with asphalt roofing cement, especially at chimney and vent-stack seams. Apply the cement using a small mason's trowel and smooth the contours of the cement so that it does not form hollows and ridges where water may collect and lead to leaks or

damage. Where you find holes of 1-square-inch or more, cut a patch from the same material as the flashing, 1 inch larger all around than the hole. Apply cement to the damaged flashing, press the patch into place, then cover the entire area with cement and smooth the surface.

Repointing flashing

Where flashing meets brickwork it is usually embedded in mortar. Separations here require immediate repair since the loose flashing actually collects water and funnels it down beneath the roof where it may spread and do considerable damage. To repair, provided the flashing itself is sound, rake out the old mortar from the seam to a

depth of about ¾ inch. Press the flashing back into place, wedging it if necessary with small stones, then fill the seam with fresh mortar, using a trowel. Smooth the seam carefully. Seal the flashing with asphalt roofing cement after the mortar has fully cured. If the flashing is corroded or damaged, you will have to replace it.

Rake out joint and repoint with fresh mortar

Galvanic action

Corrosion Table
1. Aluminum
2. Zinc
3. Steel
4. Tin
5. Lead
6. Brass
7. Copper
8. Bronze

Metals touching each other react when wet. As a result, metal flashing must be fastened with nails made of the same metal as the flashing, otherwise one or the other will corrode, often quickly. If it is impossible to match flashing and fasteners, use neoprene or asphalt washers with the fasteners to prevent direct contact between the two different metals. The chart shows

commonly-used construction metals. When paired, metals farthest apart in the series corrode soonest and fastest. Metals in contact with certain acid-containing woods such as redwood and red cedar can also corrode. When purchasing flashing, exterior wood shingles or siding, and fasteners to match, ask your building-materials supplier for advice.

REPLACING CHIMNEY FLASHING

Chimney flashing is usually in two parts: the base (or step) flashing, which wraps completely around the base of the chimney and extends several inches under the roof covering, and the cap (or counter) flashing, which covers the top edges of the base flashing. Sometimes roofing felt extends up the sides of the chimney, taking the place of metal base flashing.

To replace, carefully chisel out the mortar joints securing the cap flashing and remove it. Then chisel the joints further, to a depth of 1½ inches. Remove any roof shingles or other covering overlapping the base flashing, and carefully pry it free. Use the old flashing as patterns to cut new pieces, preferably from copper sheet sold for the purpose. Bend the flashing to shape after cutting, then fasten it in place using asphalt roofing cement. Attach the front piece of base flashing first, then the sides. Fasten the back piece last.

Refasten or replace the shingles after attaching the base flashing. Then install the cap flashing (follow the same order—front, sides, back) and seal all the joints with fresh mortar where appropriate, and roofing cement.

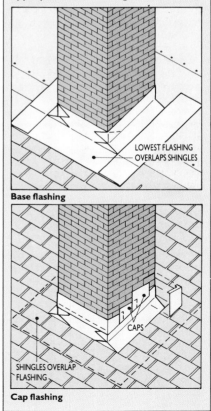

LOWEST FLASHING OVERLAPS SHINGLES

Base flashing

CAPS

SHINGLES OVERLAP FLASHING

Cap flashing

Flashing a vent stack

Sometimes you may be able to stop leaks by tightening the lead collar (if present) around the neck of the pipe where it passes through the roof. To do this, tap with a screwdriver or blunt mason's chisel and a hammer around the upper rim of the collar, sealing it against the stack. Also try coating the entire flashing area and lower portion of the vent stack with roofing cement.

To apply new flashing if repair is not possible, first remove the shingles covering the old flashing. In some cases you then may be able merely to slip a new piece of flashing over the old one and replace the roofing. Otherwise, pry up the old flashing as well, place a new piece of felt over the existing one, install the new flashing and then re-apply the roofing. The flashing must overlap the downhill shingles yet lie underneath those uphill.

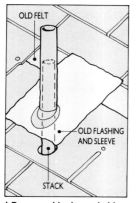

I Remove shingles and old flashing

2 Install new felt and flashing

3 Reapply shingles

Renewing valley flashing

Where shingles are trimmed so that flashing is visible, the construction is termed "open valley." In a "closed valley," shingles overlap, hiding the flashing from view.

Small repairs to open valley flashing can be made with roofing cement. Larger holes can be patched as described on page 232, provided the upper edge of the patch can be slipped beneath an overlapping piece of flashing above. Leaks from no apparent source may sometimes be stopped by applying a bead of cement between the edges of the trimmed shingles and the flashing.

To repair closed valley flashing, first try slipping squares of copper or aluminum flashing material underneath the shingles in the damaged area. Loosen or remove the nails closest to the valley, then prebend and install the squares beginning at the bottom of the roof. Overlap them until they extend 2 inches beyond the damaged area. Renail the shingles and cover the nail heads with roofing cement. If leaks persist, remove the valley shingles and install new flashing. Then replace the shingles.

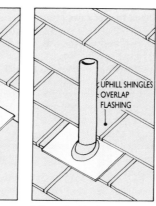

Open valley flashing

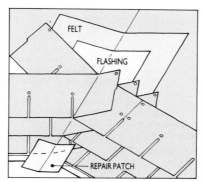

Closed valley flashing

Vertical wall flashing

A row of individual, overlapping flashing shingles are often installed where dormers join roofs and where roofs of different heights butt against each other. To locate and repair leaks in these areas, siding and roofing must be removed. Look for rotten or discolored sheathing, and evidence that settling has occurred which may have pulled house sections slightly apart. After remedying these problems, fill any gaps between building sections with strips of wood, apply new felt underlayment over the area, then reflash the area as you reshingle, by attaching a flashing shingle at the end of each course, fastened to the vertical surface with one nail at the upper corner. Each shingle should overlap the one underneath, and extend 4 inches up the vertical section and 2 inches under the roof covering. After the roofing is complete, attach new siding to cover the top edge of the flashing.

SEE ALSO	
Details for:▷	
Checking for leaks	36
Repairing roofs	37-39

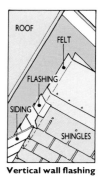

Vertical wall flashing

Drip flashing

During construction, strips of flashing are installed above doors and windows and along roof edges. These should extend several inches under the siding or roof covering and be nailed well away from the edges. On roofs, the drip edge goes on top of the underlayment along the rake and beneath it at the eaves. If minor repairs do not suffice, remove the siding or roof covering overlapping the flashing. Determine the cause of the leak, then refasten or (if necessary) replace the drip edge, cover the seams with roofing cement and reinstall the exterior material.

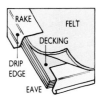

Drip edge

Repairing flat roof flashing

Felts comprising a built-up roof are generally left long at the edges and angled upward to create a raised flashing that directs water away from the edge. Cracks often develop where the angle begins. To repair, first cement down any loose flaps of roofing, then cover the area with a generous layer of roofing cement. Cut additional strips of felt, and build up the flashing by laying down alternate layers of felt and cement to obtain a smooth, even rise with no hollows that can retain water.

Flat roof

ROOF DRAINAGE

An adequate system of gutters and downspouts in good working condition is essential to maintaining the rest of the home. Gutters prevent water from running down the sides of the house, causing discoloration. Combined with downspouts, gutters also direct water away from the foundation of the building, lessening the risk of basement flooding and foundation settling. Gutters also help to prevent the washing out of flowerbeds and other landscaping around the perimeter of the house. Keeping the system working requires regular inspection and maintenance.

Gutters and downspouts

Gutters are made of a number of materials. Wood was once traditional in America, along with cast iron or copper for masonry structures. Although new homes in some regions are still built with wood gutters, in most cases galvanized sheet metal (iron), stainless steel, aluminum, fiberglass and vinyl are most common.

The size and layout of a guttering system must enable it to discharge all the water from a given roof area. The flow load required depends mainly on the area of the roof. For roofs with areas less than 750 square feet, gutters with 4-inch-wide troughs usually suffice. Choose 5-inch gutters for roofs with areas between 750 and 1400 square feet; 6-inch gutters are available for even larger roofs.

Downspouts also should be properly sized to carry away runoff adequately. For roof areas up to 1,000 square feet, 3-inch-diameter downspouts are ordinarily sufficient. Larger roofs require 4-inch-diameter spouts. The location of downspouts can affect the system's performance. A system with a central downspout can serve double the roof area of one with an end outlet. A right-angled bend in the guttering will reduce the flow capacity by about 20 percent if it is placed at a point near the outlet.

GUTTER HANGERS

Three styles of gutter-fastening hardware are popular. Although 30-inch spacing is standard, 24-inch spacing provides increased support necessary to withstand snow and ice loads.

Gutter spike is driven through gutter into fascia board. Sleeve fits in trough

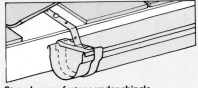

Strap hanger fastens under shingle

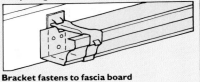

Bracket fastens to fascia board

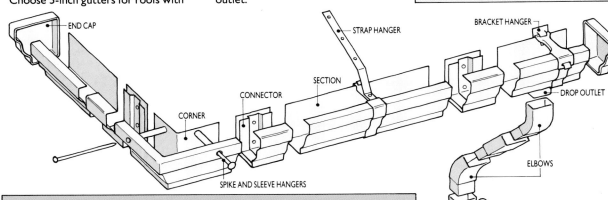

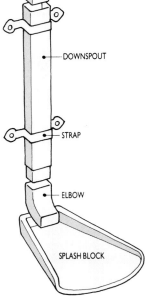

GUTTER MATERIALS

Wood gutters made of fir, redwood or red cedar (all decay-resistant) are used in some parts of the country, generally with wood-shingled roofs. Wood gutters are very sturdy and if maintained will last the life of the house.

Galvanized steel or iron gutters are often the lowest priced of all systems. Available unfinished or enameled, they have a short life compared to other materials unless frequently repainted. Paint will not adhere to galvanized metal until after one year. Use a special primer to prevent new paint from flaking.

Aluminum is very common as guttering material. Available in several enamel colors as well as unfinished it is lightweight and corrosion-resistant. However, aluminum guttering will not withstand ladder pressure. Sometimes aluminum guttering is cut and bent to shape on site. More often, systems are put together from components sold in standardized dimensions.

Plastic, especially vinyl, is becoming more popular than aluminum as gutter material. Sections and fittings are pre-colored and come in standard sizes.

Removing debris

Inspect and clean out the interiors of gutters at least twice a year (in autumn after the leaves have fallen, and again in early spring). Check more often if you live in a heavily wooded area. Use a ladder to reach the gutter. At least 12 inches should extend above the gutter to allow you to work safely.

First block the gutter outlet with a rag. Then, wearing heavy work gloves to avoid cuts, remove debris from the gutters. Scrape accumulated silt into a heap using a shaped piece of plastic or light sheet metal, then scoop it out with a garden trowel and deposit it in a bucket hung from the ladder. Sweep the gutter clean with a whisk broom, then remove the rag and flush the gutter using hard spray from a garden hose. Check whether the water drains completely or remains in standing pools, indicating a sagging gutter section.

Leaking seams where gutter sections are joined can be sealed using silicone caulk. For the best seal, disassemble the sections, apply caulk inside the seam, then reassemble the joint. Otherwise, spread caulk over the seam on the inside of the gutter, and smooth the surface to avoid producing ridges that might trap water.

If downspouts are clogged, free them using a plumber's snake or drain auger. Work from the bottom if possible, to avoid compacting debris further. If necessary, disassemble the downspout sections to get at the blockage. If downspout blockage is frequent, install leaf strainers in gutter outlets or, in severe situations, attach wire mesh leaf guards over the entire length of the gutters to slow the accumulation of debris.

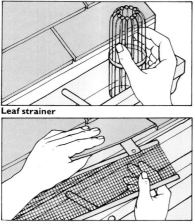

Leaf strainer

Wire mesh leaf guard

Repairing small holes

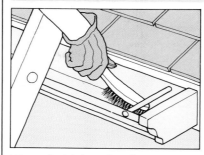

1 To repair pinholes and small rust spots
First clean the gutter and scrub the damaged area using wire brush or coarse sandpaper. Wipe away residue using a rag dipped in paint thinner.

2 Apply coat of asphalt roofing cement
On holes larger than 1/4 in., sandwich layers of heavy aluminum foil between coats of cement. Smooth top coat so water won't collect.

Patching large areas

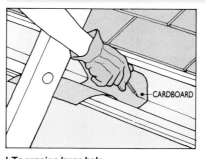

CARDBOARD

1 To repair a large hole
First use thin cardboard to make a pattern, then cut a patch of the same material as the gutter to fit over the damaged area, overlapping the hole at least 1 in.

2 Coat with asphalt roofing cement
Press the patch into place, then crimp over outer edge of gutter. Apply another layer of cement, smoothing it so water won't collect.

Maintaining wood gutters

Repaint wood gutters at least once every three years. Work during a period of warm, fair weather. First clear the gutter and allow a few days for the wood to dry thoroughly. Next, sand the interior of the gutter smooth and remove the residue with a whisk broom and hand-held vacuum. Wipe the sanded trough with paint thinner, then apply a thin coat of asphalt roofing cement mixed with paint thinner or turpentine to brushing consistency, so cement will enter wood pores. Apply a second thin coat two days later after the first has dried. Sand and repaint the gutter exterior with two coats of house paint.

Snow and ice

Plastic guttering can be badly distorted and even broken by snow and ice building up in it. Dislodge the build-up with a broom from an upstairs window if you can reach it safely. Otherwise climb a ladder to remove it.

If snow and ice become a regular seasonal problem you should screw a snow board made from 1 × 3 in. planed softwood treated with a wood preservative and painted. Fix it to stand about 1 in. above the eaves tiles, using 1 × 1/4 in. steel straps bent as required.

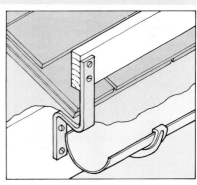

A snow board protects gutters or glazed roofs

SEE ALSO
Details for: ▷
Moisture problems   5-7

47

FITTING NEW GUTTERS AND DOWNSPOUTS

When your old gutter system reaches the end of its useful life you should replace it. Try to do so with a system in the same style or, at least, one that goes with the character of your house. If you plan to install the guttering yourself a vinyl system is probably the best choice, being easy to handle.

SEE ALSO

◁ Details for:
Moisture problems   5-7

Installing gutters

An easy way to plan a new gutter system is to make a bird's-eye view sketch of the roof, as if you were looking straight down on it. Measure the distances between corners and note the locations of existing drains. Gutter sections are usually sold in 10-foot lengths, so you'll have to make up individual runs using combinations of section-lengths and couplings. Bring your plan with you when you purchase materials and ask your supplier to help determine the parts you will need.

After determining the high and low points of each run, and the slope (see "Positioning," this page), install a gutter bracket at the high point of a run and a downspout drop outlet at the low point. Stretch a string between the two fittings, then install the intermediate brackets needed to support the gutter, spacing them no more than 30 inches apart, 24 inches being best in areas where there is normally moderate to occasionally heavy snowfall.

Assemble the gutter runs on the ground. With help from an assistant hoist them into place, then seal the ends to the drop outlets using silicone caulk for metal gutters and manufacturer-recommended sealant for the vinyl guttering system you have chosen.

Positioning

Gutter runs should not exceed 35 feet per downspout. Longer runs normally slope from the middle to a downspout at each end, but may slope instead toward a central downspout. The slope should be constant, dropping approximately ¼ inch per foot from the highest point to the downspout drop outlet.

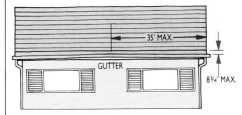

When mounting, center gutters so that roofing overlaps inner edge by half the gutter's width. The highest point of the gutter varies with the roof slope. Gutters should catch water falling vertically yet allow snow and ice to slide freely off the roof without touching the gutter to prevent damage.

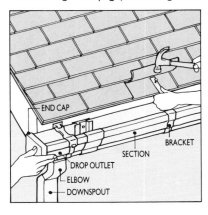

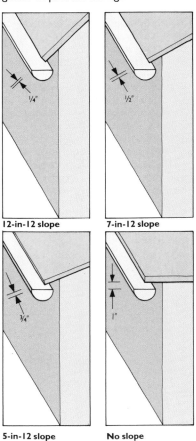

12-in-12 slope   7-in-12 slope

5-in-12 slope   No slope

Installing downspouts

Assemble downspouts from elbow sections sold for the purpose and lengths of spouting. At the top, you will have to make up a "return" that joins the spout to the drop outlet yet allows the vertical section to lie along the side of the house. At the bottom, another elbow directs the flow of water away from the foundation, into a concrete splash block or underground drain.

To install downspouts after they are assembled, slip them into place at the top but do not fasten them with cement or permanent sealer; someday they may have to be removed. Do fasten the vertical pipe to the house trim, however. Use straps designed for the job, and predrill holes in the trim if necessary to prevent splitting. Install two straps for each 10-foot vertical length of downspout pipe.

INSULATION

No matter what fuel you use, the cost of heating a home has, over recent years, risen dramatically—and there's no reason to suppose it won't continue to rise, perhaps at an even faster rate. What makes matters worse for many homeowners is the heat escaping from their drafty, uninsulated homes. Even if the expense of heating wasn't an important factor, the improved comfort and health of the occupants would more than justify the effort of installing adequate insulation.

Specifications for insulation

Homes in nearly all parrts of the United States benefit from some amount of insulation. Even in the warmest parts of the country insulation is valuable in keeping excessive heat from infiltrating living spaces and in improving the efficiency of air conditioners by preventing cooled air from rapidly escaping. Reputable insulation contractors or your local building inspector can tell you the amount of insulation recommended for your region. When comparing thermal insulating materials, you'll encounter certain technical specifications:

U-values
The building materials that are already present in your house have been rated by the construction industry and government housing authorities according to the degree to which the materials conduct heat. For individual materials, these ratings are called K-values, and represent the total heat transmitted per square foot per hour between the surfaces of two materials when there is a temperature difference between the two of 1 degree F. When the passage of heat is measured through an entire structure—such as a wall, ceiling or floor, which is made up of several different materials plus air spaces—the rating is called the U-value. The higher the U-value, the more rapidly heat passes from one surface of the structure to another.

R-values
Adding insulation reduces U-values (but not K-values) by resisting the passage of heat through a structure. The degree of resistance is termed the R-value, and it is by this rating that insulation is compared and sold. Materials with superior insulating qualities have the highest R-values.

CHOOSING INSULATION PRIORITIES

To many people, the initial outlay for total house insulation is prohibitive, even though they will concede that it is cost-effective in the long term. Nevertheless, it's important to at least begin insulating as soon as possible —every measure contributes some saving.

Many authorities suggest that 35 percent of lost heat escapes through the walls of an average house, 25 percent through its roof, 25 percent through drafty doors and windows and 15 percent through the floor. At best, this can be taken as a rough guide only as it is difficult to define an "average" home and therefore to deduce the rate of heat loss. A town house, for instance, will lose less than a detached house of the same size, yet both may have a roof of the same area and a similar condition. Large, ill-fitting sash windows will permit far more drafts than small, well-fitting casements, and so on.

The figures identify the major routes for heat loss, but don't necessarily indicate where you should begin your program in order to achieve the quickest return on your investment or, for that matter, the most immediate improvement in comfort. Start with the relatively inexpensive measures.

1 HOT-WATER HEATER AND PIPES

Begin by insulating your hot-water storage heater and any exposed pipework running through unheated areas of the house. This treatment will constitute a considerable saving in a matter of only a few months.

2 RADIATORS

Apply metallic foil behind any radiators on an outside wall. It will reflect heat back into the room before the wall absorbs it.

3 DRAFTPROOFING

Seal off the major air leaks around windows and doors. For a modest outlay, draftproofing provides a substantial return both economically and in terms of your comfort. It is also easy to accomplish.

4 ROOF

Tackle the insulation of the roof next as, in addition to the eventual reduction in fuel bills, you may be eligible for assistance towards the cost of its insulation. Insulating the roof is usually the most cost-effective major insulating task.

5 WALLS

Depending on the construction of your house, insulating the walls may be a sound investment. However, it's likely to be relatively expensive, so it will take several years to recoup your initial expenditure.

6 FLOORS

Most of us insulate our floors to some extent by laying carpets or tiles. Taking extra measures will depend on the degree of comfort you wish to achieve and whether you can install more efficient insulation while carrying out some other improvement to the floor, such as laying new boards.

7 DOUBLE GLAZING (STORM WINDOWS)

Contrary to typical advertisements, double glazing will produce only a slow return on your investment, especially if you choose one of the more expensive systems. However, it may help to increase the value of your property— a double-glazed room is definitely cozier, and you will be less troubled by noise from outside, especially if you choose to install triple glazing.

DRAFTPROOFING DOORS

A certain amount of ventilation is desirable for a healthy environment and to keep water vapor at an acceptable level; it's also essential to enable certain heating appliances to operate properly and safely. But using uncontrolled drafts to ventilate a house is not the most efficient way of dealing with the problem. Drafts account for a large proportion of the heat lost from the home and are also responsible for a good deal of discomfort. Draftproofing is easy to fit, requires no special tools, and there's a wide choice of threshold weatherstripping available to suit all locations.

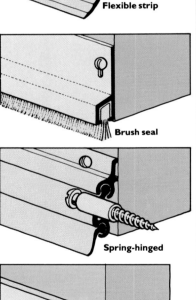

Flexible strip

Brush seal

Spring-hinged

Flexible arch

Locating and curing drafts

Test exterior doors—and windows—first, and seal only those interior doors which are the worst offenders to provide "trickle" ventilation from room to room. Check out other possible sources of drafts, such as floorboards and baseboards, fireplaces, attic hatches, and overflow pipes from plumbing fixtures.

Locate drafts by running the flat of your hand along the likely gaps. Dampening your skin will enhance its sensitivity to cold, or wait for a very windy day to conduct your search.

There are so many manufacturers and variations of threshold weatherstripping excluders, it's quite impossible to describe them all, but the following examples illustrate the principles commonly employed to seal out drafts. Choose the best you can afford, but perhaps more importantly, try to decide which type of threshold system will suit your particular requirements best.

THRESHOLD WEATHERSTRIP SYSTEMS

The gap between the door and floor can be very large and will admit fierce drafts. Use a weatherstripped threshold to seal this gap. If it is to be used on an exterior door, make sure it is suitable for this purpose. Buy a device that fits the opening exactly, or cut it to fit from a larger size.

FLEXIBLE-STRIP WEATHERSTRIPPING

The simplest form of threshold weatherstrip is a flexible strip of plastic or rubber, that sweeps against the floorcovering to form a seal. The basic versions are self-adhesive strips that are simply pressed along the bottom of the door, but others have a rigid plastic or aluminum extrusion screwed to the door to hold the strip in contact with the floor. This type of weatherstrip is rarely suitable for exterior doors and quickly wears out. However, it is inexpensive and easy to fit. Most types work best over smooth flooring.

BRUSH SEAL

A nylon bristle brush set into a metal or plastic extrusion acts as a draft excluder. It is suitable for slightly uneven or textured floorcoverings; the same excluder works on both hinged and sliding doors.

SPRING-HINGED

A plastic strip and its extruded clip are spring-loaded to lift from the floor as the door is opened. On closing the door, the strip is pressed against the floor by a stop screwed to the door frame. This is a good-quality interior and exterior weatherstripping that reduces wear on the floorcovering.

FLEXIBLE ARCH

An aluminum extrusion with a vinyl arched insert presses against the bottom edge of the door. The extrusion has to be nailed or screwed to the floor, so it would be difficult to use on a solid concrete floor. If you fit one for an exterior door, make sure it is fitted with additional under-seals to prevent the rain from seeping beneath it. You may have to plane the bottom of the door.

DOOR KITS

The best solution for an outside door is a kit combining an aluminum weatherstrip, which sheds the rainwater, and a threshold with a built-in tubular rubber or plastic draft excluder. Components can be purchased individually or as a package.

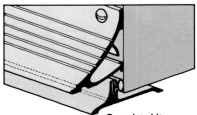

Complete kit

WEATHERSTRIPPING THE DOOR EDGES

Any well-fitting door requires a gap of ¹/₁₆ inch at top and sides so that it can be operated smoothly. However, the combined area of a gap this large loses a great deal of heat. There are several ways to seal it, some of which are described here. The cheaper varieties have to be renewed regularly.

FOAM STRIPS

The most straightforward weatherstrip is a self-adhesive foam plastic strip, which you stick around the rabbet and is compressed by the door, forming a seal. The cheapest polyurethane foam will be good for one or two seasons (but it's useless if painted) and is suitable for interior use only. Better-quality vinyl-coated polyurethane, rubber or PVC foams are more durable and do not deteriorate on exposure to sunlight, as their cheaper counterparts do. Don't stretch foam weatherstripping when applying it, as it reduces its efficiency. The door may be difficult to close at first but the stripping soon adjusts.

SEE ALSO

Details for:▷
Weatherstripping doors   21

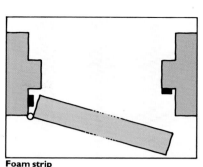
Foam strip

FLEXIBLE TUBE

A small vinyl tube held in a plastic or metal extrusion is compressed to fill the gap around the door. The cheapest versions have an integrally molded flange, which can be stapled to the door frame, but they are not as neat.

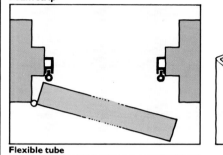

Flexible tube

SPRING STRIP

Thin metal or plastic strips with a sprung leaf are pinned or glued to the door frame. The top and closing edges of the door brush past the leaf, which seals the gap, while the hinged edge compresses it. It can't cope with uneven surfaces unless it incorporates a foam strip on the flexible leaf.

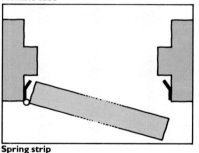
Spring strip

V-STRIP

A variation on the spring strip, the leaf is bent right back to form a V-shape. The strip can be mounted to fill the gap around the door or attached to the door stop so that the door closes against it. Most are cheap and unobtrusive.

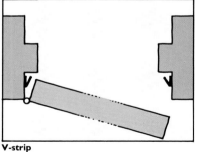

V-strip

SEAM SEALANT

With this method, a wad of rubberized sealant can be pressed into the door frame. Squeeze a wad of sealant onto the doorstop, then cover it with low-tack masking tape. Close the door, which will flatten the wad and force sealant against the door frame. Then remove the tape, leaving the sealant firmly attached.

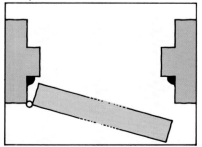

Sealant

SEALING KEYHOLES AND LETTERBOXES

Make sure the outer keyhole for a mortise lock is fitted with a pivoting coverplate to seal out drafts in the winter.

Special hinged flaps are made for screwing over the inside of a letterbox. Some types contain a brush seal behind the flap, forming an even better seal.

Keyhole coverplate
The coverplate is part of the escutcheon.

Letterbox flap
A hinged flap neatens and draftproofs a letterbox.

GENERAL DRAFTPROOFING

Hinged casement windows can be sealed with any of the draft excluders suggested for fitting around the edge of a door, but draftproofing a sliding sash window presents a more difficult problem.

Sealing a sash window

The top and bottom closing rails of a sash window can be sealed with any form of compressible weatherstripping; the sliding edges admit fewer drafts but they can be sealed with a brush seal fixed to the frame—inside for the lower sash, outside for the top one.

A spring or V-strip could be used to seal the gap between the central meeting rails, but you may not be able to reverse the sashes once it is fitted. Perhaps the simplest solution is to seal it with a reusable tubular plastic strip.

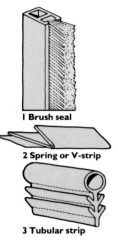

I Brush seal

2 Spring or V-strip

3 Tubular strip

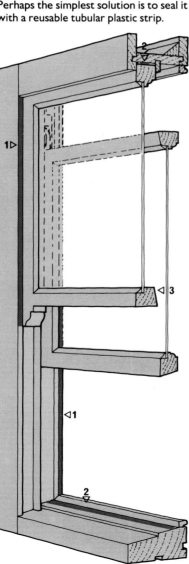

Clear liquid sealer

If you plan never to open a window during the winter, you could seal all gaps with a clear liquid draft seal, applied from a tube. It is virtually invisible when dry and can be peeled off, without damaging the paintwork, when you want to open the window again after the winter.

Liquid sealer is supplied in a special injector

Sealing a pivot window

As you close a pivot window, the moving frame comes to rest against fixed stops, but the stops for the top half of the window are on the outside of the house. These exterior stops, at least, must be sealed with draft excluders that are weatherproof, so use spring or V-strip compressible weatherstripping, or a good-quality flexible tube strip. Alternatively, use a draftproofing sealant.

DRAFTY FIREPLACES

A chimney can be an annoying source of drafts. If the fireplace is unused, you can seal it off completely, but be sure to fit a ventilator to provide ventilation for the flue.

If you want to retain the appearance of an open fireplace, cut a sheet of thick polystyrene to seal the throat but leave a hole about 2 inches across to provide some ventilation. Should you ever want to use the fireplace again, don't forget to remove the polystyrene, which is flammable.

DRAFTPROOFING FLOORS AND BASEBOARDS

The ventilated crawlspace below a wooden first floor is a prime source of drafts through gaps in the floorboards and between the wall and the baseboard. The best solution is to install fiberglass insulation beneath the floorboards. Seal the gap between the baseboard and the floor with caulk applied with an applicator gun or in the form of quarter-round strips. For a neat finish, pin molding to the baseboard to cover the sealed gap.

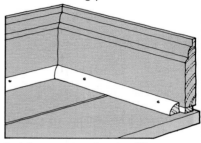

Seal the gap with caulk and molding

DRAFTPROOFING A DRYER VENT

An open dryer vent leading to the outside of the house can be a significant source of drafts both in winter and during windy weather. If yours is an electric dryer, check with a heating expert about the possibility of connecting the dryer vent to the furnace return duct, thus saving the heat generated by the dryer which is otherwise wasted by being expelled through the vent. Do not vent the dryer directly into the laundry area; dryer air is damp and you risk an indoor condensation problem. Gas dryers should remain vented to the outdoors.

To seal off the dryer vent permanently or for occasional use, merely disconnect the flexible dryer exhaust pipe from the wall opening and pack the opening with fiberglass insulation (enclose the insulation in a small muslin sack if it is to be removed often). Remove the insulation and reconnect the pipe each time you use the dryer.

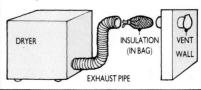

INSULATING ROOFS

About a quarter of the heat lost from an average house goes through the roof, so preventing this should be one of your priorities when it comes to insulating your home. Providing you're able to gain access to your attic floor, reducing substantial heat loss is just a matter of laying the insulation material between the joists: It's cheap, quick and effective. If you want to use the attic, insulating the sloping surface of the roof is a quite straightforward alternative.

Treating a flat roof

A flat roof—on an extension, for instance—may also need insulating, but since blowing in insulation between the rafters from outside may endanger overhead wiring and fixtures, the only really practical solution for most homeowners is to apply a layer of insulation to the ceiling surface, or remove the existing ceiling, insulate, then install a new ceiling. Installing ceiling tiles is an alternative, but their insulation value is minimal.

Preparing the attic

On inspection, you may find that the roof space has existing but inadequate insulation. It is worth installing extra insulation to bring it up to the recommended R-value rating for your climate region. Check roof timbers for pest damage or signs of rot so that they can be treated first. Make sure that the electrical wiring is sound; lift it clear so that you can lay insulation beneath it.

Plaster or plasterboard ceiling surfaces will not support your weight, so lay a plank or two, or a panel of chipboard, across the joists so that you can move about safely. Don't allow it to overlap the joists; if you step on the edge it will tip over.

If there is no permanent lighting in the attic, rig up a "trouble" light on an extension cord, so you can move it wherever it is needed, or hang it high up for best overall light.

Most attics are very dusty, so wear old clothes and a paper respirator. You may wish to wear protective gloves, particularly if you are handling fiberglass batts or blanket insulation, which can irritate sensitive skin.

TYPES OF INSULATION

There's a wide range of different insulation materials available. Assess your requirements and study the options before purchasing.

BLANKET INSULATION

Fiberglass and mineral- or rock-fiber blanket insulation is commonly sold as rolls made to fit snugly between the joists. The same material cut to shorter lengths is also sold as "batts." A minimum thickness of 3½ inches is recommended for attic insulation. Blanket insulation may be unbacked, paper-backed to improve its tear-resistance, or have a foil backing as a vapor barrier (see below).

The unbacked type is normally used for laying on the attic floor. Blankets are 2 to 6 inches thick and typically 15 inches wide—suitable for the normal 16-inch joist spacing. For wider-than-usual joist spacing, choose the 23-inch width (cut in half with a panel saw before you unwrap it for narrow joist spaces). Rolls are sold by square-foot area. Blankets are usually sold in 4-foot lengths.

If you want to fit blanket insulation to the sloping part of the roof, make sure it has a lip of backing along each side for stapling to the rafters.

Both fiberglass and mineral fibers are nonflammable and proofed against moisture, rot and vermin.

LOOSE-FILL INSULATION

Loose-fill insulation in pellet or granular form is poured between the joists on the attic floor to a minimum depth of 3½ inches, although a depth of 5½ inches is recommended for the same value of insulation as 3½-inch-thick blanket—but this could rise above some joists.

Exfoliated vermiculite, made from a mineral called mica, is the most common form of loose-fill insulation, but others such as mineral wool, polystyrene or cork granules may be available. Loose-fill is sold in bags containing enough material to cover a nominal 25 square feet to a depth of 4 inches.

It's inadvisable to use loose-fill in a drafty, exposed attic, because high winds can cause it to blow about. However, it's convenient to use if the joists are irregularly spaced.

BLOWN INSULATION

Professional contractors can provide interjoist attic insulation by blowing glass, mineral or cellulose fibers through a large hose. A minimum, even depth of 4 inches is required. Blown fiber insulation may be unsuitable for a house in a windy location, but seek the advice of a contractor.

RIGID INSULATION

Boards made of foamed plastic—polystyrene and polyurethane—are extremely efficient insulators. Most lumberyards and building supply stores stock them in 4 × 8-foot sheets, in thicknesses of ¾ to 2 inches. Rigid insulation is easy to install where framing is level and uniform. Fire codes require that it has a minimum ½-inch-thick fireproof covering.

VAPOR BARRIERS

Installing insulation has the effect of making the areas of the house outside that layer of insulation colder than before, so increasing the risk of condensation either on or within the structure itself. In time this could result in decreased value of the insulation and may promote a serious outbreak of dry rot in the house framing.

To prevent this from happening, it's necessary to provide adequate ventilation for those areas outside the insulation or to install a vapor barrier on the inner, or warm, side of the insulation to prevent moisture-laden air from passing through. This is usually a plastic sheet or layer of metal foil. Foil vapor barrier sometimes makes up the backing of blanket or batt insulation. The vapor barrier must be continuous and undamaged or its effect is greatly reduced.

SEE ALSO

Details for:▷

Condensation	8-9
Wet and dry rot	11
Roof ventilation	65-66

R-VALUES FOR COMMON INSULATION MATERIALS

Material	Approx. R-Value (per inch)
Fiberglass	3.5
Mineral fiber	3.5
Cellulose	3.7
Polystyrene (beadboard)	4.0
Polystyrene (extruded)	5.0
Polyurethane	7.0
Isocyanurate	7.5

● **Ventilating the attic**
Laying insulation between the joists increases the risk of condensation in an unheated roof space above, but, provided there are vents at the eaves and/or ridge, there will be enough air circulating to keep the attic dry.

53

INSULATING THE ATTIC

Laying blanket insulation

Seal gaps around pipes, vents or wiring entering the attic from outdoors with flexible caulk. Remove the blanket wrapping in the attic (it's compressed for storage and transportation but swells to its true thickness when released) and begin by placing one end of a roll into the eaves, vapor-barrier side down. Make sure you don't cover the ventilation gap—trim the end of the blanket to a wedge shape so it does not obstruct the airflow, or fit eaves vents.

Unroll the blanket between the joists, pressing it down to form a snug fit. If the roll is slightly wider than the joist spacing, allow it to turn up against the timbers on each side.

Continue at the opposite side of the attic with another roll. Cut it to butt up against the end of the first one, using a razor-knife or long-bladed pair of scissors. Continue across the attic until all the spaces are filled. Cut the insulation to fit odd spaces.

Do not cover the casings of any light fittings which protrude into the attic space. Avoid covering electrical cables, as there's a risk it may cause overheating. Instead, lay the cables on top of the blanket, or clip them to the sides of the joists above it.

If you have an attic cistern, do not insulate beneath it; heat rising from the room below will help to prevent freezing. Cut a piece of insulation to fit the hatch cover and attach it with glue. Fit foam weatherstripping around the edge of the hatch.

Laying loose-fill insulation

Take similar precautions against condensation to those described for blanket insulation. If the attic is poorly ventilated, install a polyethylene-sheet vapor barrier directly on top of the ceiling and joists. To prevent blocking the eaves, wedge strips of plywood or thick cardboard between the joists. Pour insulation between the joists and distribute it roughly with a broom. Level it with a spreader cut from hardboard to fit between the joists.

To insulate the entrance hatch, screw battens around the outer edge of the cover, fill with granules and nail on a hardboard lid to contain them.

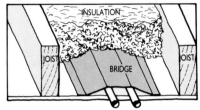

Insulating pipes between the joists

Double-thick blankets

You can install fiberglass insulation that is thicker than the height of the joists. First slash the vapor-barrier backing of the top layer of insulation every few inches, then lay it over the bottom layer at right angles to the existing layer. Take care not to block vents in the eaves.

INSULATING AROUND A CHIMNEY

Wood framing around a chimney should be 2 inches from masonry on all sides to avoid a fire hazard. To insulate, remove backing from fiberglass insulation and hand-pack area between framing and masonry.

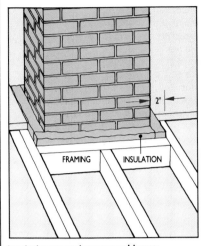

Insulating around masonry chimney

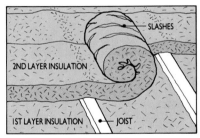

Installing new batts over old ones

Insulating around ceiling light fixtures
Leave 3-in. space on all sides surrounding recessed ceiling light fixture to avoid fire hazard. Frame around fixture to prevent loose fill from creeping.

Right
Seal gaps around pipes and vents (1). Place end of roll against eaves and trim ends (2) or fit eaves vents (3). Press rolls between joists (4).

Far right
Seal gaps to prevent condensation (1). Stop insulant from blocking ventilation with strips of plywood (2) or eaves vents (3). Cover cold water pipes with a cardboard bridge (4), then use a spreader to level the insulant (5). Insulate and draftproof the hatch cover (6).

Laying blanket insulation in the attic

Spreading loose-fill insulation in the attic

INSULATING A SLOPING ROOF

Insulating between the rafters

If the attic is in use, you will need to insulate the sloping part of the roof in order to heat the living space. Repair the roof covering first, as not only will leaks soak the insulation, but also it will be difficult to spot them after insulating.

Condensation is a serious problem when you install insulation between the rafters, as the underside of the sheathing will become very cold. You must provide a 1½-inch gap between the tiles and the insulation to promote sufficient ventilation to keep the space dry, which in turn determines the maximum thickness of insulation you can install. The ridge and eaves must be ventilated and you should include a vapor barrier on the warm side of the insulation, either by fitting foil-backed blanket or by stapling sheets of polyethylene to the lower edges of the rafters to cover unbacked insulation.

Whatever insulation you decide on, you can cover the rafters with sheets of plasterboard as a final decorative layer. The sizes of the panels will be dictated by the largest boards you can pass through the hatchway. Use plasterboard nails or screws to hold the panels against the rafters, staggering the joints. Alternatively, fit solid insulation between the rafters, with a vapor barrier and plasterboard over that, to meet fire code requirements.

Attaching blanket insulation

Unfold the side flanges from a roll of foil-backed blanket and staple them to the underside of the rafters. When fitting adjacent rolls, overlap the edge of the vapor barrier to provide a continuous layer.

Attaching solid insulation

The simplest method of attaching solid insulation is to cut the panels accurately so they wedge-fit between the rafters. If necessary, screw furring to the sides of the rafters to which you can fix the insulating sheets. Allow a 1½-inch air space. Staple a polyethylene sheet vapor barrier over the rafters. Double-fold the joints over a rafter and staple in place.

INSULATING AN ATTIC ROOM

If an attic room was built as part of the original dwelling, it will be virtually impossible to insulate the pitch of the roof unless you are prepared to remove the old plaster and proceed as left. It may be simpler to insulate from the inside as for a flat roof, but your headroom may be seriously hampered.

Insulate the short vertical wall of the attic from inside the crawlspace, making sure the vapor barrier faces the inner, warm side of the partition. Insulate between the joists of the crawlspace at the same time.

Fit blankets with vapor barrier facing the room

Insulating a room in the attic
Surround the room itself with insulation but leave the floor uninsulated so that the room benefits from rising heat generated by the space below.

Insulating an attic from the inside
Fit blanket or sheet insulation between the rafters.
1 Minimum of 1½ in. between insulation and roof for ventilation
2 Blanket or batts
3 Vapor barrier with double-folded joints stapled to rafters
4 Solid insulation fixed to battens
5 Plasterboard fastened over vapor barrier

55

INSULATING ABOVE RAFTERS

Installing insulation between the rafters and the roof covering results in a more complete thermal envelope because it avoids thermal bridging—the loss of heat from inside the house by conduction through the rafters (which are not covered by insulation). Insulating this way is best done during new construction. Before retrofitting, carefully compare the costs of this method of insulating vs. results with an insulation contractor or home-energy analyst.

Treatment over covered rafters

Where rafters are covered from view by ceiling material attached underneath, first lay down rigid foam insulation across the top surfaces of the rafters. Place strips of 1 × 2 lumber on top of the insulation, directly over the rafters, then, using nails which will penetrate at least 2 inches through the 1 × 2 strips into the rafters, fasten the insulation by nailing through the strips and insulation into the rafters. Attach roof decking over the insulation by nailing into the wood strips. Before installing the ceiling, staple sheets of polyethylene vapor barrier across the undersides of the rafters.

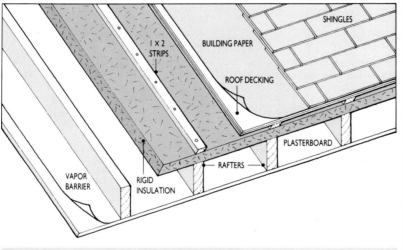

Treatment over exposed rafters

Where rafters are exposed, place insulation on top of the decking above. First lay down sheets of polyethylene vapor barrier. Then position rigid insulation on top, and nail through the insulation into the decking above the rafters. Cover the insulation with building paper before installing roof covering (no further decking is required).

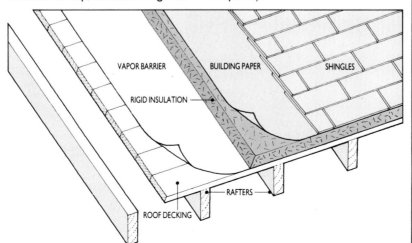

INSULATING WALLS

Although a great amount of heat escapes through the walls of a house, installing insulation in finished walls can be more expensive than the savings returned in decreased energy bills. If no insulation exists in the walls, plan on a payback period of from 5 to 10 years, the shorter time if you live in a cold climate, the longer time if you live where winters are moderate to mild. If the walls already contain some insulation, it is probable that the cost of adding more would not be offset by energy savings except over a very long period, perhaps as long as you own the home. Consult an insulation contractor and home-energy analyst for advice. If your home is completely uninsulated, check with local building authorities about the possibility of qualifying for municipal grants to help defray insulation expenses.

Options

In new construction or if you are considering major renovation, installing fiberglass-blanket insulation between the wall studs is the most common and generally the most practical method. The thickness of the insulation you'll be able to install depends upon the width of the lumber used for the studs, although by combining blanket insulation with additional insulation such as rigid foam or insulated vinyl siding applied to the exterior of the house, necessary R-values can be achieved. A typical stud-framed wall built with 2 × 4 lumber and finished on the inside with plasterboard and on the outside with wood siding already has an R-value of 5 to 7. Adding 3½-inch-thick fiberglass to that wall increases the R-value to approximately R-12.

With finished walls, common practice is to have a professional drill holes through the exterior sheathing and then blow loose-fill insulation into the cavities between the studs, using special pumping equipment.

If you are planning or prepared to re-side exterior walls, consider adding rigid insulation over the existing sheathing before re-siding. Nail the insulation to the bare sheathing, seal the seams between sheets with duct tape, apply caulk where the insulation meets any trim, then install the new siding. You'll have to increase the depth of door and window trim so it meets the siding properly. To do so, attach strips of molding around the edges, the same thickness as the insulation.

Installing fiberglass blankets

Choose insulation wide enough to fit tightly between wall studs. To cut, unroll insulation backing-side down, then use a framing square or straight-edged board to compress the insulation and act as a cutting guide. Cut the insulation 2 inches longer than the bay, using a utility knife. Afterward, pull the backing away from the fiberglass at each end to create 1-inch stapling tabs.

Press the insulation into each bay, with the backing facing toward the room. With foil-backed material, staple the tabs to the inside faces of the studs so the insulation is recessed at least ¾ inch. With paper-backed material, staple the tabs flat along the outer edges of the studs, leaving no recess. Fit insulation behind obstructions, such as pipes and electrical boxes, so it lies against the exterior sheathing. Pack unbacked insulation into gaps between window and door frames.

After installation is complete, staple polyethylene vapor barrier across the entire wall, allowing plastic to extend a few inches all around (to be covered later by finish floor, ceiling, and adjacent wall covering). Carefully cut out around windows, outlet boxes, and other openings before attaching interior wall covering.

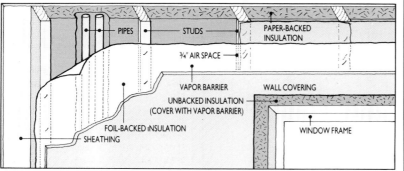

Details for installing batt insulation

Insulating masonry walls

Above ground, masonry walls can be insulated with either blanket or rigid insulation. Below ground, because blanket insulation is susceptible to moisture damage, only rigid foam is recommended. (If you live in an extremely cold climate, insulating basement walls can cause foundation damage. Be sure to check with a local building inspector before proceeding.)

To apply blanket insulation, first cover the masonry surface with polyethylene vapor barrier, attaching it with dabs of construction adhesive. Then construct an ordinary stud wall against the masonry (nailing it to the floor and ceiling) and pack the bays with insulation as described on this page. Cover the insulation with a second vapor barrier before finishing with plasterboard or paneling.

To install rigid insulation, first attach a vapor barrier to the masonry as described, then power-nail vertical 1 × 2 furring strips to the wall, spaced 16 inches apart on center. Press insulation panels into the bays between strips—they should fit snugly—then cover the wall with vapor barrier and the finished wall covering, fastened to the furring strips.

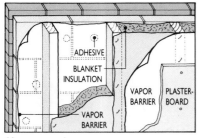

Above-ground masonry

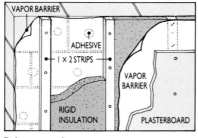

Below-ground masonry

INSULATING A HOT-WATER HEATER

One of the least expensive, most effective energy-savers possible is to insulate your hot-water heater. Hardware and home-supply stores sell inexpensive kits containing precut fiberglass insulation for wrapping around hot-water tanks of various sizes. It's also easy to make your own water-heater insulating jacket. Cut strips of paper-backed fiberglass insulation materials (the thicker the better), wrap them horizontally around the heater and fasten them with strips of duct tape. Wrap insulating foam tubes around pipework, especially the hot-water outlet pipe. Leave the thermostat, pressure relief valve and control knobs exposed. On gas- or oil-fired heaters, cut the insulation to stop 2 inches from the vent stack (which usually connects to the furnace piping) and air intake (usually located at the base of the tank). Leave these areas exposed as well.

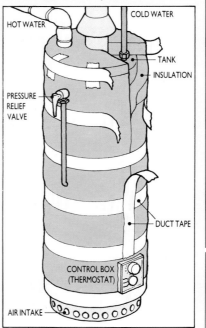

Insulating a hot-water heater
Fit insulation snugly around the tank and wrap insulating foam tubes around the pipework, especially the hot-water outlet pipe.

SAFETY

Fiberglass and mineral wool can severely irritate skin, lungs, eyes and mucous membranes. When handling, always wear long sleeves and trousers, gloves, goggles and a respirator.

INSULATING A FLOOR

Even with carpet or other covering above, heat can readily escape through the ground floor into an unheated basement or crawlspace below.

Floors are best insulated from underneath, by pressing fiberglass or mineral wool insulation between the floor joists, much the same way as in insulating a stud-frame wall. Foil-backed insulation is the best choice, since it reflects escaping heat back in the direction from where it came. Because joists are normally wider than wall studs, greater thicknesses of insulation may be used. Insulation may be pressed snugly against the subfloor (allow a ¾-inch gap if using foil-backed insulation), or be fastened level with the bottom edges of the joists. Be sure the insulation extends over the foundation sills at the ends of the joists. This is a primary heat-loss area.

No matter whether you use foil- or paper-backed insulation, the backing, which acts as a vapor barrier, must face the warm living space above. This makes fastening the insulation in place difficult, because the tabs on each side are no longer accessible. One solution is to staple wire mesh such as chicken wire across the joist edges as you install the insulation. The other—recommended especially if a basement ceiling must be installed—is to cut lengths of stiff wire each slightly longer than the distances between joists, and press them up at 18- to 20-inch intervals into each bay to hold the insulation in place above.

Insulating from below
To secure insulation between floor joists either staple wire mesh to lower edges of joists (right) or press lengths of heavy wire between joists (far right).

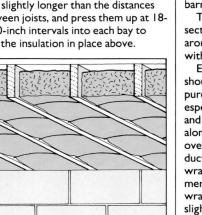

Crawlspaces

It is seldom necessary to fully insulate crawlspaces, provided insulation is installed beneath the house floor above. A polyethylene vapor barrier should be spread over the crawlspace floor and extended at least part way up the walls to prevent moisture buildup, and the space itself should be adequately vented to the outside. The vapor barrier may be left exposed if the space is unused.

Should insulation be required, proceed as for insulating a masonry wall or by merely draping fiberglass or mineral-wool blankets down from the foundation top. Anchor the insulation with bricks along the top, and with bricks or a length of lumber at the bottom.

Batt insulation for crawlspace

AIR DUCTS AND PIPES

Hot-air ducts running through unheated basements or crawlspaces should be insulated to prevent heat loss, unless such loss is desirable to warm the space. Also, ducts carrying air from central air-conditioning systems should be insulated to retain cool air if they pass through areas that are not air-conditioned. Fiberglass and mineral-wool blanket insulation, with and without a reflective vapor barrier, is sold for this purpose at heating and air-conditioning supply stores. Choose reflective-barrier insulation for air-conditioning ducts. Ordinarily, no barrier is needed for hot-air ducts.

To install the insulation, cut it into sections where necessary, wrap it around the duct, then secure the seams with duct tape.

Exposed steam and hot-water pipes should also be insulated. For these, purchase foam insulation sleeves sold especially for the purpose at plumbing and hardware stores. The sleeves are slit along one side. To install, slip the sleeve over the pipe, then seal the seam with duct tape. Insulated, adhesive pipe wrapping is also available. To attach this, merely remove the backing paper, then wrap the tape in a spiral, overlapping it slightly around the pipe along its entire exposed length.

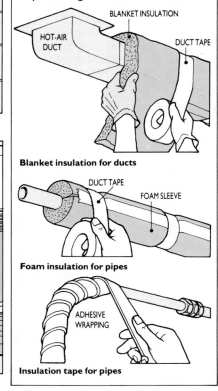

Blanket insulation for ducts

Foam insulation for pipes

Insulation tape for pipes

DOUBLE GLAZING

A double-glazed window consists of two sheets of glass separated by an air gap. The air gap provides an insulating layer, which reduces heat loss and sound transmission. Condensation is also reduced because the inner layer of glass remains relatively warmer than that on the outside. Factory-sealed units and secondary glazing are the two methods in common use for domestic double glazing. Both will provide good thermal insulation. Sealed units are unobtrusive, but secondary glazing can offer improved sound insulation. But which do you choose to suit your house and your lifestyle?

What size air gap?

For heat insulation, a ¾-inch gap provides the optimum level of efficiency. Below ½ inch, the air can conduct a proportion of the heat across the gap. Above ¾ inch, there is no appreciable extra gain in thermal insulation and air currents can occur, which transmit heat to the outside layer of glass. A larger gap of 4 to 8 inches is more effective for sound insulation. A combination of a sealed unit plus secondary glazing provides the ideal solution, and is known as triple glazing.

Double glazing will help to cut fuel bills, but its immediate benefit will be felt by the elimination of drafts. The cold spots associated with a larger window, particularly noticeable when sitting relatively still, will also be reduced. In terms of saving energy, the heat lost through windows is relatively small—around 10 to 12 percent—compared to the whole house. However, the installation of double glazing can halve this amount.

Double glazing will improve security against forced entry, particularly if sealed units, tempered or wired glass have been used. However, make sure that some accessible part of the window is openable to provide emergency escape in case of fire.

SEE ALSO

Details for: ▷
Secondary glazing   60

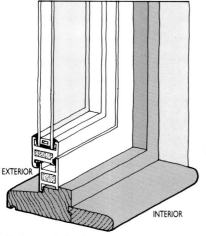

Factory-sealed unit
A complete frame system installed by a contractor.

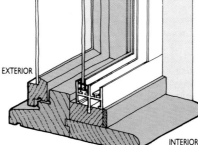

Secondary window system
Fitted in addition to the normal glazed window.

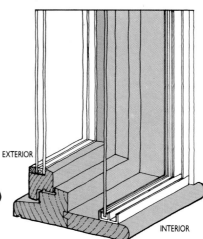

Triple glazing
A combination of secondary and sealed units.

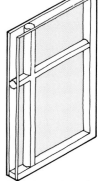

Georgian sealed unit

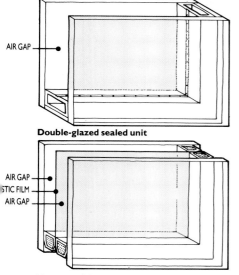

Double-glazed sealed unit

Heat-retentive sealed unit

Double-glazed sealed units

Double-glazed sealed units are manufactured from two panes of glass separated by a spacer and hermetically sealed all around. The cavity between the glass may be ¼, ⅜, ½ or ¾ inch wide. The gap may contain dehydrated air to eliminate condensation between the glass, or inert gases which also improve thermal and acoustic insulation.

The thickness and type of glass is determined by the size of the unit. Clear float glass or tempered glass is common. When obscured glazing is required for privacy, patterned glass is used. Special heat-retentive sealed units are also supplied by some double glazing companies, incorporating special glass or a plastic film embodied within the unit.

For period-style windows, a leaded light and a Georgian version of the sealed unit are also produced. The former is made by bonding strips of lead to the outer pane of the glass, the latter by placing a molded framework of glazing bars in the cavity. The improved security, lack of maintenance and ease of cleaning in some way make up for their lack of character, compared with the original style of window.

Generally, these special sealed units are produced and installed by suppliers of ready-made double-glazed replacement windows. Sealed units are available for do-it-yourself installation or they can be installed by the window contractor to order by specialists. Square-edged units are made for frames with a deep rabbet, and stepped units for frames intended for single glazing.

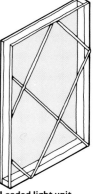

Leaded light unit

SECONDARY DOUBLE GLAZING

GLAZING POSITIONS

Secondary double glazing comprises a separate pane of glass or plastic sheet which is normally fitted to the inside of existing single-glazed windows. It is a *popular method for double glazing windows, being relatively easy for home installation—and usually at a fraction of the cost of other systems.*

Secondary double glazing is particularly suitable for DIY installation, partly because it is so versatile. It is possible to fit a system to almost any style or shape of window.

How the glazing is mounted

Glazing can be fastened to the sash frames (**1**), the window frames (**2**), or across the window reveal (**3**). The choice depends on the ease of installation, the type of glazing and personal requirements for ventilation.

Glazing fixed to the sash will cut down heat loss through the glass and provide accessible ventilation, but it will not stop drafts. That flxed to the window frame will reduce heat loss and stop drafts at the same time. Glazing fixed across the reveal will also offer improved sound insulation, as the air gap can be wider. Any system should be readily demountable or preferably openable to provide a change of air in a room without some other form of ventilation.

Rigid glazing of plastic or glass can be fitted to the exterior of the window opening if secondary glazing would spoil the appearance of the interior. In this case, windows which are set in a deep reveal, such as the vertically sliding sash type, are the most suitable (**4**).

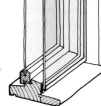

1 Sash-mounted
Glazing fixed to the opening window frame

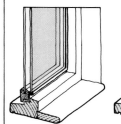

2 Frame-mounted
Glazing fixed to the structural frame

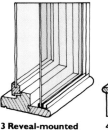

3 Reveal-mounted
Glazing fixed to the reveal and interior windowsill

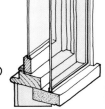

4 Exterior-fitted
Glazing fixed to the reveal and exterior windowsill

Glazing with renewable film

Effective double glazing kits are available which consist of double-sided adhesive tape and thin plastic sheet to stretch across the window frame. Both can be removed at the end of the cold season without harming the paintwork.

Clean the window frame (**1**), then cut the plastic sheet roughly to size, allowing an overlap all around. Apply double-sided tape to the frame edges (**2**) and peel off its backing paper.

Attach the film to the top rail (**3**), then tension it onto the tape on the sides and bottom of the frame (**4**). Apply light pressure only until the film is positioned then rub it down onto the tape all around.

Use a hair dryer set to a high temperature to remove all creases and wrinkles in the film (**5**). Starting at an upper corner, move the dryer slowly across the film, holding it about ¼ inch from the surface. When the film is tensioned, cut off the excess plastic (**6**).

1 Wipe woodwork to remove dust and grease

2 Apply double-sided tape to the fixed frame

3 Stretch the film across the top of the frame

4 Pull the film tight and fix to sides and bottom

5 Use a hair dryer to shrink the film

6 Trim the waste with a sharp knife

PLASTIC GLAZING

Demountable systems

A simple method for interior secondary glazing uses clear plastic film or sheet. These lightweight materials are secured by self-adhesive strips or rigid molded sections, which form a seal. Most strip fastenings use plastic tracks or some form of rententive tape, which allows the secondary glazing to be removed for cleaning or ventilation. The strips and tapes usually have a flexible foam backing, which takes up slight irregularities in the woodwork. They are intended to remain in place throughout the winter and be removed for storage during the summer months.

Fitting a demountable system

Clean the windows and the surfaces of the window frame. Cut the plastic sheet to size. Place the glazing on the window frame and mark around it (1). Working with the plastic on a flat table, peel back the protective paper from one end of the self-adhesive strip. Tack it to the surface of the plastic, flush with one edge. Cut it to length and repeat on the other edges. Cut the mating parts of the strips and apply them to the window frame following the guidelines. Press the glazing into place (2).

When dealing with rigid molded sections, cut the pieces to length with mitered corners. Fit the sections around the glazing, peel off the protective backing and press the complete unit against the frame (3).

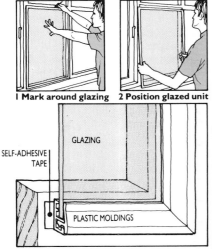

1 Mark around glazing   **2 Position glazed unit**

3 Rigid plastic moldings support the glazing

PLASTIC MATERIALS FOR DOUBLE GLAZING

For economy and safety, plastic sheet materials can be used in place of glass to provide lightweight double glazing. They are available in clear thin flexible films or clear, textured and colored rigid sheets.

Unlike glass, plastic glazing has a high impact-resistance and will not splinter when broken. Depending on thickness, plastic can be cut with scissors, drilled, sawn, planed and filed.

The clarity of new plastics is as good as glass but they will scratch. They are also liable to degrade with age and are prone to static. Plastic sheet should be washed with a liquid soap solution. Slight abrasions can be rubbed out with metal polish.

Film and semirigid plastics are sold by the square foot or in rolls. Rigid sheets are available in a range of standard sizes or can be cut to order. Rigid plastic is covered with a protective film of paper on both faces that is peeled off only after cutting and shaping to keep the surface scratch-free.

POLYESTER FILM

This is a plastic film used for inexpensive double glazing. Polyester film can be trimmed with scissors or a knife and fixed with self-adhesive tape or strip fasteners.

It is a tough, virtually tearproof film, which is very clear—ideal, in fact, for glazing living rooms. It is sold in rolls and is available in several widths and thicknesses.

POLYSTYRENE

This material is a relatively inexpensive clear or textured rigid plastic. Clear polystyrene does not have the clarity of glass and will degrade in strong sunlight. It should not be used for south-facing windows or where a distortion-free view is required. Depending on climatic conditions, the life of polystyrene is reckoned to be between three and five years. However, its working life can be extended if the glazing is removed for storage in summer. Polystyrene is available in several thicknesses and sheet sizes.

ACRYLIC

A good-quality rigid plastic with the clarity of glass. It costs about the same as glass and about half as much again as polystyrene. Its working life is considered to be at least 10 years. Acrylic is also available in a wide range of translucent and opaque colors. It is available in several thicknesses and sheet sizes.

POLYCARBONATE

A relatively new plastic glazing material, which is virtually unbreakable. It provides a lightweight vandal-proof glazing with a high level of clarity. The standard grade costs about twice the price of acrylic. It is made in clear, tinted, opal and opaque grades, some with textured surfaces. Thicknesses suitable for domestic glazing are $1/16$, $1/8$ and $5/32$ inch, although greater thicknesses are made, some in grades which are even bulletproof. Several sheet sizes are also available.

PVC GLAZING

PVC is available as a flexible film or as a semirigid sheet. The film provides inexpensive glazing where a high degree of clarity is not required, such as in a bedroom. PVC is ultraviolet-stabilized and is therefore suitable for outside or inside use. Consequently, it is very suitable for glazing sunspaces (and carport roofs). Several sheet sizes are available.

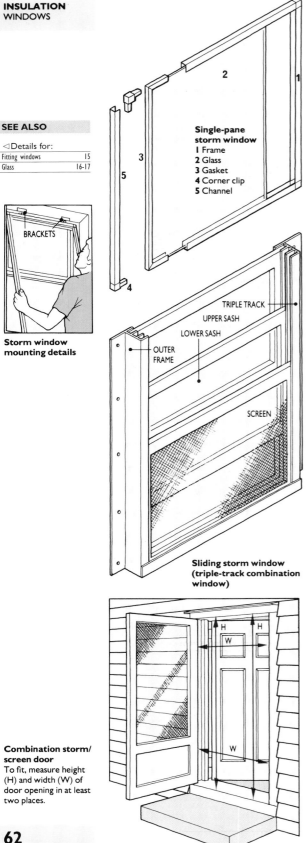

**Storm window
mounting details**

**Single-pane
storm window**
1 Frame
2 Glass
3 Gasket
4 Corner clip
5 Channel

**Sliding storm window
(triple-track combination
window)**

**Combination storm/
screen door**
To fit, measure height
(H) and width (W) of
door opening in at least
two places.

STORM GLAZING SYSTEMS

Secondary glazing applied to the exterior of windows usually takes the form of storm sashes, either one-piece, single-plate windows which are installed in the fall and taken down in spring, or permanently mounted sliding-sash panes which remain in place all-year-round. Single-plate storm windows can be homemade, often at considerable savings over purchased windows. However, sliding windows are best left to professional storm-window installers.

How to make a single-pane storm window

Measure the length and width of the window opening by holding the tape against the outside edges of the blind stop against which the storm window will seat. Single-pane storm window kits are often available at hardware and building supply stores and home centers. If you can't find a kit in the size you need, purchase lengths of aluminum storm-window channel (prefitted with U-section rubber glazing gasket), and friction-fit corner clips (usually sold with the channel) to make the frame. Don't attempt to make windows taller than 5 feet, because such large areas of glass are hard to handle.

Remove the gasket, then cut four pieces of channel so that when assembled, the outside dimension of the frame measures 1/8 inch less in both height and width than the window opening.

Assemble three sides of the frame using the corner clips to hold the pieces together. Drive the clips into the channel-ends using a small ball-peen hammer.

Purchase double-strength glass for the pane, cut so it will fit between the channels of the frame with the gasket installed. Fit the gasket around the edge of the pane, mitering the gasket sides at each corner with a utility knife (discard the triangular scraps of waste gasket), then slide the pane into the frame and install the final length of channel.

Attach two-piece storm-window hanging brackets from the top edge of the storm window, then mount the window to the outside of the opening. The storm window should seat firmly. However, you may wish to fasten it at the bottom and apply removable weatherstripping around the inside.

Sliding storm windows

Sliding storm windows, usually called double- or triple-track combination windows (because they incorporate a screen for use during summer), are available from home and building supply centers. Most often they are designed to fit the outside of double-hung window frames, and can be operated merely by raising the interior window to gain access to the latches controlling each sash. In triple-track units, the upper storm window sash is mounted—sometimes permanently—in the outermost track of the storm-window frame. The lower sash slides up and down in the middle track, and a screen slides up and down in the innermost track. In double-track units, the lower sash and screen are interchangeable, to be switched according to season.

It is important that sliding storm windows are well-made and tight-fitting. When purchasing, look for quality corner construction, gasketing on both sides of the glass, and deep tracks in the channel. Metal latches are more durable than plastic ones. At the bottom of each frame should be small (1/4-inch-diameter) holes to prevent condensation. When having storms installed, be sure caulk is applied to the existing frame before the storm frame is mounted. See that the windows operate smoothly before accepting the job.

Combination storm and screen doors

Combination storm doors are most often available made of aluminum. However, wood doors offer greater energy savings. Both are usually sold mounted in a frame, ready for installation. To measure the door opening, measure both the height and the width in at least two places. Use the smallest measurement in each case. For the height, measure between the door sill and the inside face of the top of the door frame or brick mold. For the width, measure between the two outermost offsets (rabbets) in the side pieces of the door frame. Usually, there must also be at least 1 inch of flat surface on the door frame boards or brick mold outside the door in order to mount the storm-door frame.

VENTILATION

Ventilation is essential for a fresh, comfortable atmosphere, but it has a more important function with regard to the structure of our homes. It wasn't a problem when houses were heated with open fires, drawing fresh air through all the natural openings in the structure. With the introduction of central heating, insulation and draftproofing, well-designed ventilation is vital. Without a constant change of air, centrally heated rooms quickly become stuffy, and before long the moisture content of the air becomes so high that water is deposited as condensation—often with serious consequences.

There are various ways to provide ventilation. Some are extremely simple, while others are much more sophisticated for total control.

Initial consideration

Whenever you undertake an improvement which involves insulation in one form or another, take into account how it is likely to affect the existing ventilation. It may change conditions sufficiently to create a problem in those areas outside the habitable rooms so that moisture and its side effects develop unnoticed under floorboards or in the attic. If there is a chance that damp conditions might occur, provide additional ventilation.

Ventilating wall cavities

Faulty vapor protection can lead to moisture accumulating within walls. The problem is common in renovated houses where insulation has been retrofitted into the original construction. Suspect the need for ventilation especially if you notice paint blisters on the exterior of the house.

To ventilate wall cavities, install vent plugs—small cylindrical louvers available in several diameters from hardware and building-supply stores. Drill holes from the exterior of the house into each cavity where moisture is suspected, at the bottom, top, and at 4-foot intervals in between, and insert the plugs.

Ventilating a fireplace

An open fire needs oxygen to burn brightly. If the supply is reduced by thorough draftproofing or double glazing, the fire smolders and the slightest downdraft blows smoke into the room. There may be other reasons why a fire burns poorly, such as a blocked chimney, for example, but if it picks up within minutes of partially opening the door to the room, you can be sure that inadequate ventilation is the problem.

One efficient and attractive solution is to cut holes in the floorboards on each side of the fire and cover them with a ventilator. Cheap plastic grilles work just as well, but you may prefer brass or aluminum for a living room. Choose a "hit-and-miss" ventilator, which you can open and close to seal off unwelcome drafts when the fire is not in use. If the room is carpeted, cut a hole in it and screw the ventilator on top into the floor.

Another solution is to install a sealed fireplace door unit, which comes with inlet pipes and a small blower. Cut holes in the exterior wall at each side of the fireplace, insert the pipes, and attach vents on the outside.

Ventilating an unused fireplace
An unused fireplace that has been blocked by brickwork, blockwork of plasterboard should be ventilated to allow air to flow up the chimney to dry out penetrating dampness or condensation. Some people believe a vent from a warm interior aggravates the problem by introducing moist air to condense on the cold surface of the brick flue. However, so long as the chimney is uncapped, the updraft should draw moisture-laden air to the outside. A brick vent installed in the flue from outside is a safer solution but it is more difficult to accomplish and, of course, impossible if the chimney is located within the house. Furthermore, the vent would have to be blocked should you want to reopen the fireplace later.

To ventilate from inside the room, leave out a single brick, form an aperture with blocks, or cut a hole in the plasterboard used to block off the fireplace. Screw a face-mounted ventilator over the hole or use one that is designed for plastering in. The thin flange for screw-fixing the ventilator to the wall is covered as you plaster up to the slightly protruding louver.

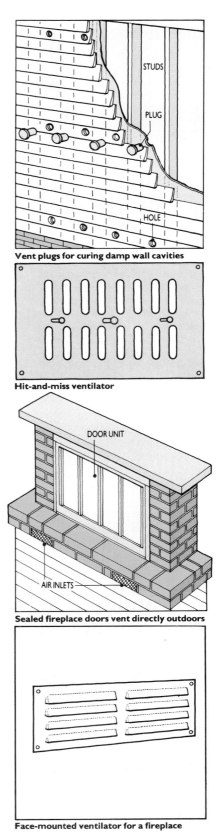

Vent plugs for curing damp wall cavities

Hit-and-miss ventilator

Sealed fireplace doors vent directly outdoors

Face-mounted ventilator for a fireplace

63

VENTILATING CRAWLSPACES

Because of their confined area, and because both cold and dampness are particularly likely to invade crawlspaces, ventilating them adequately is crucial. Whether the above-ground foundation walls are brick or block, louvered ventilators should be built into them on at least two opposite sides. If none are present, or if the number of ventilators seems inadequate, add additional ones or replace those existing with larger ones. Keep ventilators open except in inclement weather. Occasionally, vents become clogged with leaves or other debris.

Single ceramic brick vent

Double plastic brick vent

Assessing existing ventilation

Ideally, there should be a brick vent every 6 feet along an external crawlspace wall, but in many buildings there is less provision for ventilation with no ill-effects. Sufficient airflow is more important than the actual number of openings.

Pockets of noncirculating air in corners where drafts never reach are particularly prone to harboring the microorganisms which create dry rot. Frequently, these corners also are where the ends of floor joists rest on sills and against headers, which only increases the likelihood that moisture problems will eventually set in unless plenty of fresh air is kept flowing through the area.

If you suspect poor circulation in specific areas of a crawlspace, fit additional brick vents in the walls nearby, placing two vents at right angles, if possible, to create a cross-draft.

When checking the condition of existing vents, also be aware that even small holes can admit vermin unless screened over. Don't be tempted to block the opening. If you can't fix screen across it, or if the vent is damaged, replace it.

Installing or replacing a brick vent

Use a masonry drill to remove the mortar and a cold chisel to chop out the masonry you are replacing. You may have to cut some blocks to install a double-size vent. Having cut through the wall, spread mortar on the base of the hole and along the top and both sides of the new vent. Push it into the opening, keeping it flush with the face of the masonry. Repoint the mortar to match the profile used on the surrounding wall.

Installing brick vents
Brick vents or other louvered ventilators can be installed either by replacing foundation masonry or by cutting through the joist header that rests on the sill.

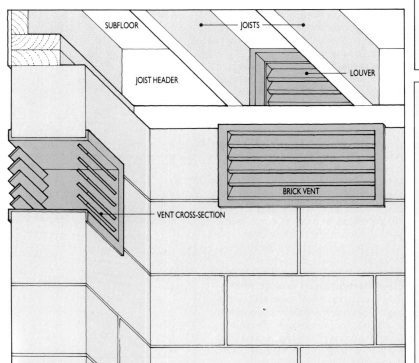

SUBFLOOR — JOISTS
JOIST HEADER
LOUVER
BRICK VENT
VENT CROSS-SECTION

VENTING A CAVITY WALL

If you build a vent into a brick cavity wall, bridge the gap with a plastic, telescopic unit, which in turn is mortared into the hole from both sides. If necessary, a louver can be screwed to the inner end of the telescopic unit. Where a vent is inserted above the damp-proof course, you must fit a cavity tray over the telescopic unit to stop water from running to the inner leaf of the cavity wall.

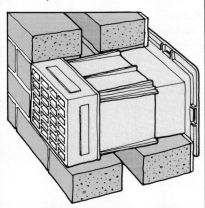

Brick vent with telescopic sleeve
Bridge a cavity wall with this type of unit.

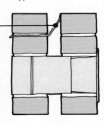

Cavity tray
A galvanized cavity tray sheds any moisture which penetrates the cavity above the unit to the outer leaf of the wall. It is necessary only when the vent is fitted above the damp-proof course.

VENTING AN APPLIANCE

A flued, fuel-burning appliance must have an adequate supply of air to function efficiently and safely. If any alteration or improvement interferes with that supply, you must provide alternative ventilation. If you plan to block a vent, change the window or even install an exhaust fan in the same room as the appliance, consult a professional installer. He will tell you whether the alteration is advisable, what type and size of vent to install, and where it should be positioned for best effect. An appliance with a balanced flue draws air directly from outside the house, so will be unaffected by internal alterations.

VENTILATING THE ROOF SPACE

When insulating the attic first became popular as an energy-saving measure, homeowners were recommended to tuck insulation right into the eaves to keep out drafts. What people failed to recognize was the fact that the free flow of air is necessary in the colder roof space to prevent moisture-laden air from the dwelling below from condensing on the structure. Inadequate ventilation can lead to serious deterioration. Wet rot develops in the roof timbers and water drops onto the insulation, eventually saturating the material and rendering it ineffective as insulation. If water builds up into pools, the ceiling below becomes stained and there is a risk of short-circuiting the electrical wiring in the attic. Efficient ventilation of the roof space, therefore, is an absolute necessity for every home.

Ventilating the eaves

Building codes specify ventilation requirements, so check with a building inspector before installing vents yourself. One rule of thumb for estimating the amount of ventilation necessary is 1 square foot each of intake and outflow ventilation for every 300 square feet of roof.

The configuration of ventilators most suitable depends primarily on the amount of air that needs to circulate and the way in which the rafter ends are enclosed by the rest of the roof framing. Most sloping roofs incorporate vent plugs or strips installed in the soffit beneath the eaves for intake and gable-end louvers at each end of the house for outflow. In cases where gable-ends are not accessible, the peak of the roof can be opened and a ridge vent installed along its length. Other types of vents are designed for installation on some part of the sloping roof itself.

Installing eaves vents

In most houses where soffit vents do not already exist, installing vent plugs rather than strips is usually recommended. First, determine the locations of the rafter ends. Then, in the spaces between them, drill holes for the vents and apply caulk to their edges to prevent decay. Install the vents themselves by pressing them into place. Each plug should incorporate a screen to keep out pests. If necessary, install baffles between the rafters to prevent insulation from blocking airflow underneath the roof.

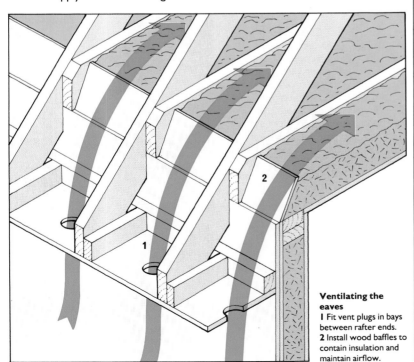

Ventilating the eaves
1 Fit vent plugs in bays between rafter ends.
2 Install wood baffles to contain insulation and maintain airflow.

COMMON VENT PATTERNS

Because warm air rises, air entering at eaves level is most effectively vented at the ridge. However, there are cases where vents must be located elsewhere on the roof.

Eave vents and gable-end louver
This is the most common arrangement for pitched-roof buildings.

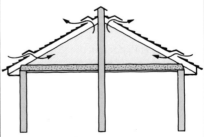

Ridge vent
Where gable ends are inaccessible or nonexistent—as on a hipped roof—a continuous ridge vent provides sufficient outflow ventilation.

Pitched-roof vents
For venting special roof areas or when usual ventilation points are inaccessible, install pitched-roof vents. Place vents as high as possible to replace ridge vents, as low as possible to vent eaves.

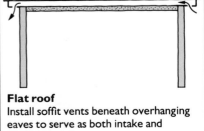

Flat roof
Install soffit vents beneath overhanging eaves to serve as both intake and outflow ventilators.

Soffit vent plug

Pitched-roof vent

Turbine vent

FITTING ROOF VENTS

Installing a ridge vent

A continuous ventilating strip running the length of the roof provides very effective outflow ventilation. Ridge venting may be installed on any pitched roof, during new construction or reroofing, or as a task by itself.

If a ridge vent is to be included in the new construction of a roof, the roof decking is laid to leave a gap on either side of the ridge board, creating an open slot along the roof peak approximately 2 inches wide. Determine the actual width from the size of the ridge vent. The gap allows exiting air to pass through. If felt roofing paper is laid, trim it even with the top edge of the decking. Fasten the ridge vent over the gap, nailing it into the decking and rafters on both sides. Lay the final course of shingles on each side of the roof so that they cover the base of the vent.

To install a ridge vent to a finished roof, you will have to cut a gap along the roof peak to create a passage for exiting air. Use a chalk line to mark the cutting line on each side of the peak, then cut through the shingles and felt paper first, using a linoleum knife, to expose the decking. Set the blade of a circular saw to the thickness of the decking, then cut along each chalked line to open the roof. Be careful to avoid nails; also be sure not to cut into the rafters.

Caulk the underside of the ridge vent sides, then fasten it over the slot using gasketed roofing nails long enough to penetrate the rafters.

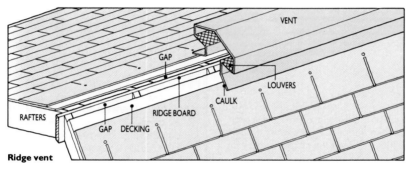

Ridge vent

Installing pitched-roof ventilators

Installing ventilators on the sloping portions of a roof requires careful cutting and sealing to prevent leaks. You may wish to hire a professional roofer to do the job.

First, determine the location of the vent. It must lie between rafters. Use the vent itself or a template made of cardboard (sometimes supplied with the vent) to mark the area of the roof to be cut out. It should be smaller than the overall dimensions of the vent base so that the vent can be slid beneath adjacent shingles. Cut out the area by first removing the roof covering (use a linoleum knife to remove asphalt shingles), then sawing through the decking using a saber saw. Apply roofing cement to the underside of the vent. Then slide it into place and fasten it with galvanized roofing nails while, at the same time, holding neighboring shingles up and out of the way. Cover the nail heads with more cement, then smooth the shingles surrounding the vent so they lay flat.

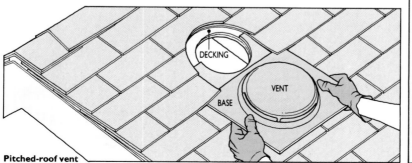

Pitched-roof vent

CALCULATING AIRFLOW CAPACITY

All vents positioned near the eaves should provide the equivalent of at least 1-inch continuous gap, depending on the pitch of the roof. The ones near the ridge should provide airflow to suit the construction of a particular roof.

Divide the specified airflow capacity of the vent you wish to use into the recommended continuous gap to calculate how many vents you will need. If in doubt, provide slightly more ventilation than is indicated.

Place eaves vents in the fourth or fifth course of shingles, slates or tiles. Position the higher vents a couple of courses below the ridge. Space all vents evenly along the roof to avoid any areas of "dead" air.

CLEARING THE OPENING

When replacing certain tiles or slates with a vent, it may be necessary to cut through a tile support strip to clear the opening. Nail a short length of wood above and below the opening to provide additional support.

Because roofing slates overlap each other by a considerable amount, you will have to cut away the top corners of the lower slates.

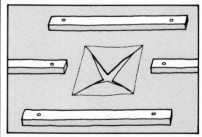

Providing additional support
Cut a strip that obstructs a hole, then place strips above and below to support the vent.

Marking the slates that obstruct the hole
When slates cover the opening for a vent, use a template to mark the corners, then remove them.

FITTING AN EXHAUST FAN

Kitchens and bathrooms are particularly susceptible to problems of condensation so it is especially important to have a means of efficiently expelling moisture-laden air along with unpleasant odors. An electrically driven exhaust fan will freshen a room faster than relying on natural ventilation and without creating uncomfortable drafts.

Positioning an exhaust fan

The best place to site a fan is either in a window or on an outside wall, but its exact position is more critical than that. Stale air extracted from the room must be replaced by fresh air, normally through the door leading to other areas of the house. If the fan is sited close to the source of replacement air it will promote local circulation but will have little effect on the rest of the room.

The ideal position would be directly opposite the source as high as practicable to extract the rising hot air (1). In a kitchen, try to locate the fan adjacent to the stove but not directly over it. In that way, steam and cooking smells will not be drawn across the room before being expelled (2). If the room contains a flued, fuel-burning appliance, you must ensure there is an adequate supply of fresh air at all times or the exhaust fan will draw fumes down the flue. The only exception is an appliance with a balanced flue, which takes its air directly from outside.

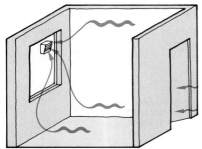

1 Fit exhaust fan opposite replacement air source

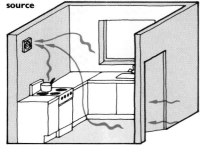

2 Place fan near a stove in a kitchen

Types of exhaust fans

Many fans have integral switches but, if not, a switched connection unit can be wired into the circuit when you install the fan. Some models incorporate built-in controllers to regulate the speed of extraction and timers to switch off the fan automatically after a certain time. Fans can be installed in a window and some, with the addition of a duct, will extract air through a framed or solid wall (see illustrations below). Choose a fan with external shutters that close when the fan is not in use, to prevent backdrafts.

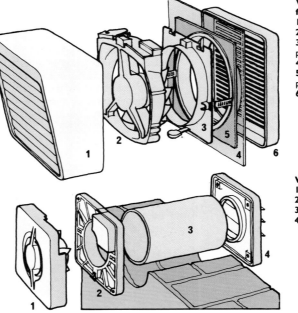

Window-mounted fan
1 Inner casing
2 Motor assembly
3 Interior clamping plate
4 Glass
5 Louver clamping plate
6 Exterior grille

Wall-mounted fan
1 Motor assembly
2 Interior backplate
3 Duct
4 Exterior louver

Choosing the size of a fan

The size of a fan, or to be accurate, its capacity, is determined by the type of room in which it is installed and the volume of air it must move.

A fan installed in a kitchen must be capable of changing the air completely ten to fifteen times per hour. A full bathroom requires fifteen to twenty air changes per hour and a powder room, ten to fifteen. A living room normally requires four to six changes per hour, but fit a fan with a slightly larger capacity in a smoky environment.

To calculate the capacity of the fan you require, find the volume of the room (length × width × height), then multiply that figure by the recommended number of air changes per hour. Choose a fan which is capable of the same or slightly higher capacity.

SEE ALSO

Details for: ▷
Condensation 8-9
Range hoods 69

CALCULATING THE CAPACITY OF A FAN FOR A KITCHEN

SIZE			
Length	**Width**	**Height**	**Volume**
11 ft.	10 ft.	8 ft.	880 cu. ft.

AIR CHANGES		
Per hour	**Volume**	**Fan capacity**
15	880 cu. ft.	13,200 cu. ft.

Metal detector
Detect buried pipes or cables by placing an electronic sensor against the wall.

I Hold panel with plank

2 Seal plate fitting

3 Insert duct in hole

4 Attach louver

FITTING A WALL-MOUNTED UNIT

Satisfy yourself that there is no plumbing or wiring buried in the wall by looking in the attic or under the floorboards. Make sure there are no drainpipes or other obstructions.

Cutting the hole

Wall-mounted fans are supplied with a length of plastic or metal ducting for inserting in a hole which you must cut through the wall to the outside. Plot the center of the hole and draw its diameter on the inside of the wall. Use a long-reach masonry drill to bore a central hole right through. Be sure to hold the drill perpendicular to the wall. To prevent the drill from breaking out brickwork or stucco on the outside, press a thick plywood panel against the wall and wedge it with a scaffold board supported by stakes in the ground (1).

Insert a keyhole saw or saber saw in the center hole, then saw around the inside of the planned opening to remove most of the waste plasterboard. If necessary, trim the hole larger using a rasp. Saw through the exterior wall from the outside, using the same method. Keep the hole small enough so that its edges will be hidden by the fan mounting plate and exterior louver.

Fitting the fan

Most wall fans are fitted in a similar manner, but check specific instructions. Separate the components of the fan. If necessary, attach a self-adhesive foam sealing strip on the fitting on the backplate to receive the duct (2).

Insert the duct in the hole so that the backplate fits against the wall (3). Mark the length of the duct on the outside, allowing enough extra to fit the similar fitting on the outer louver. Cut the duct to length with a hacksaw. Reposition the backplate and duct to mark the mounting holes on the wall. Drill the holes, then feed the electrical supply cable into the backplate before screwing it to the wall. Stick a foam sealing strip inside the fitting on the louver. Position it on the duct, then mark and drill the wall mounting holes. Use a screwdriver to stuff scraps of fiberglass insulation between the duct and the cut edge of the hole, then screw on the exterior louver (4).

If the louver does not fit flush with the wall, seal the gap with caulk. Wire the fan and attach the motor assembly to the backplate.

FITTING AN EXHAUST FAN

Installing a fan in a window

Some fans are designed to fit in fixed windows. If you wish to fit one in a sash window, it's necessary to secure the top sash in which the fan is installed and fit a sash stop on each side of the window to prevent the lower sash from damaging the casing of the fan should it be raised too far.

To install an exhaust fan in an hermetically sealed double glazing system, ask the manufacturer to supply a special unit with a hole cut and sealed around its edges to receive the fan. Some manufacturers supply a kit which adapts a fan for installing in a window with secondary double glazing. It allows the inner window to be opened without dismantling the fan.

Cutting the glass

A window-mounted fan requires a round hole to be cut in the glass. The size is specified by the manufacturer. It is possible to cut a hole in an existing window but stresses in the glass will sometimes cause it to crack, and while the glass is removed for cutting there is always a security risk, especially if you decide to take it to a glazier. All things considered, it is advisable to fit a new pane; it's easier to cut and can be installed immediately once the old one has been removed.

Cutting a hole in glass is not easy; it may be more economical in the long run to order it from a glazier. You'll need to supply exact dimensions, including the size and position of the hole. Use strengthened glass in a thickness recommended by the fan manufacturer or glazier.

Installing the fan

The exact assembly may vary but the following sequence is a typical example of how a fan is installed in a window. Take out the existing window pane and clean up the frame, removing traces of old putty and glazier's points. Fit the new pane, with its hole precut, as for fitting window glass.

From outside, fit the exterior louver by locating its circular flange in the hole (1). Attach the plate on the inside, which clamps the louver to the glass. Tighten the mounting screws in rotation to achieve a good seal and an even clamping force on the glass (2). Screw the motor assembly to the clamping plate (3). Wire up the fan following the maker's instructions. Fit the inner casing over the motor assembly (4).

I Place louver in the hole from outside

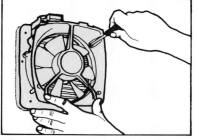

3 Screw the motor assembly to the plate

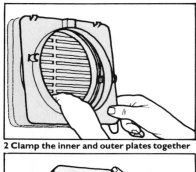

2 Clamp the inner and outer plates together

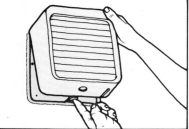

4 Attach the inner casing to cover the assembly

> **WARNING**
>
> **Never make electrical connections until the power is switched off at the service panel.**

INSTALLING A RANGE HOOD

Window- and wall-mounted fans are designed for overall room extraction, but the ideal way to tackle steam and greasy cooking smells from a stove is to mount a specially designed exhaust hood directly over it.

Where to mount the range hood

Mount a range hood between 2 and 3 feet above the stovetop or about 1 foot 4 inches to 2 feet above an eye-level grill. Unless the manufacturer provides specific dimensions, mount a hood as low as possible within the recommended tolerances for best results.

Depending on the model, a range hood may be cantilevered from the wall or, alternatively, screwed between or beneath kitchen cupboards. Some kitchen manufacturers produce a stove hood housing unit, which matches the style of the cupboards. Opening the unit operates the fan automatically. Most range hoods have two or three speed settings and a built-in light fitting to conveniently illuminate the stovetop below.

Installing ductwork

When a range hood is mounted on an outside wall, air is extracted through the back of the unit into a straight duct passing through the rear wall. If the stove is situated against another wall, it is possible to connect the hood with the outside by means of fire-resistant ductwork. Straight and curved components plug into each other to form a continuous shaft running along the top of the wall cupboards, then through the wall.

Plug the female end of the first duct component over the outlet fitting on the top of the range hood. Cutting them to fit with a hacksaw or multisnips, run the rest of the ductwork, making the same female-to-male connections along the shaft. Some ducting is printed with airflow arrows to make sure each component is oriented correctly. If you were to reverse a component somewhere along the shaft, air turbulence might be created around the joint, reducing the effectiveness of the extractor. At the outside wall, cut a hole and fit an external louver to finish the job (see opposite).

Fitting a range hood

Recycling and extracting hoods are hung from wall brackets supplied with the machines. Screw mounting points are provided for attaching them to wall cupboards. Cut a ducting hole through a wall as for a wall-mounted fan (see opposite). Wire a range hood following the maker's instructions.

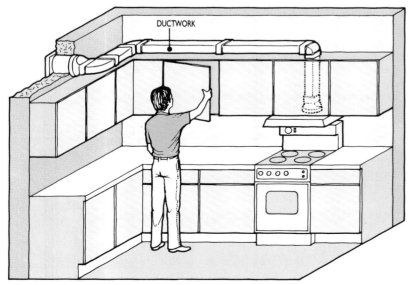

DUCTWORK

RECIRCULATION OR EXTRACTION?

The only real difference between one range hood and another is the way it deals with the stale air it captures. Some hoods filter out the moisture and grease before returning the freshened air to the room. Other machines dump stale air outside through a duct in the wall, just like a conventional wall-mounted exhaust fan.

Because the air is actually changed, extraction is the more efficient method, but it is necessary to cut a hole through the wall and, of course, the heated air is lost—excellent in hot weather but rather a waste in winter. Range hoods which recycle the air are much simpler to install but never filter out all the grease and odors, even when new. It is essential to clean and change the filters regularly to keep the hood working at peak efficiency.

SEE ALSO

Details for: ▷

| Condensation | 8-9 |

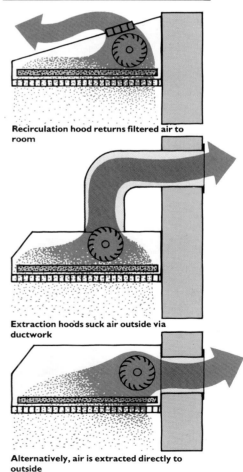

Recirculation hood returns filtered air to room

Extraction hoods suck air outside via ductwork

Alternatively, air is extracted directly to outside

◄ **Running ducts outside**
When a stove is placed against an inside wall, run ductwork from the extractor hood along the top of wall-hung cupboards.

HEAT-EXCHANGING VENTILATORS

Most people naturally think of ventilating a room in hot weather when it is most likely to be unpleasantly stuffy. In all but the hottest of summers, it can be achieved simply by opening windows or using a mechanical fan. However, ventilation is equally important in the winter—but we keep our weatherstripped windows closed against drafts, promoting an unhealthy atmosphere and a rise in condensation.

Using a conventional exhaust fan solves the problem, but at the cost of throwing away heated air. A heat-exchanging ventilator is the answer. Two centrifugal fans operate simultaneously, one to suck in fresh air from the outside while the other extracts the same volume of foul air from inside. The system is perfectly balanced so the unit works efficiently.

The benefits of a heat exchanger

An important plus for heat-exchanging ventilators is that heat loss is cut to a minimum by passing the extracted air through a series of small vents sandwiched between similar vents containing cold outside air moving in the other direction. Most of the heat is transferred to the fresh air so it is blown into the room warmed.

If you want to install a heat exchanger in a kitchen or bathroom, check that the unit is suitable for steamy atmospheres and greasy air.

Heat exchangers are either wall-mounted much like a standard extractor fan, or flush-mounted so that the cabinet housing the unit is set into the wall. A slim, louvered casing is visible only from inside. The former version is relatively simple to fit but more obtrusive. To install a flush-mounted unit, it is necessary to cut a large rectangular hole through the wall and, in some cases, frame it with lumber.

How the ventilator functions
Hot, stale air is drawn into the unit (**1**), by a centrifugal fan (**2**). It is passed via the heat exchanger (**3**) to the outside (**4**). Fresh air is sucked from outside (**5**) by a fan (**6**) to be warmed in the heat exchanger and passed into the room (**7**).

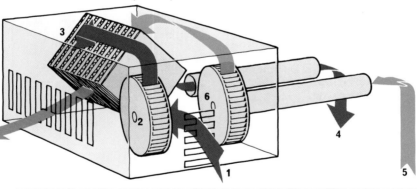

Fitting a wall-mounted ventilator

With the aid of a level, use the manufacturer's template to mark the position of the ventilator on the wall, including the centers of both ducts (**1**). Locate the unit high on the wall but with at least 2-inch clearance above and to the sides.

The ducting is likely to be narrower than that used for standard exhaust fans, so it may be possible to use a hole saw (**2**). Drill a pilot hole through both the interior wall covering and exterior sheathing and siding first. After cutting the hole in the interior wall, cut the hole in the exterior wall slightly lower so that the ducting will slope to drain condensation to the outside. If the ducting is too large to use a hole saw, use a keyhole or saber saw instead, and trim the holes using a rasp and file. Use a

hacksaw to cut the ducting to a length equaling the depth of the wall plus ⅜ inch. Use aluminum flashing tape to hold ducting to both fittings on the rear of the wall-mounting panel. Insert the ducting into the drilled holes (**3**), push the panel against the wall and mount it with screws.

Outside, plug the gaps around the ducting with fiberglass insulation (**4**) and screw the covers over the ends of the ducts. Seal around the edges of both covers with caulk (**5**). Fit the main unit to the mounting panel on the inside wall (**6**) and wire it to a fused connection box nearby.

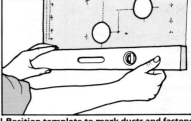

1 Position template to mark ducts and fasteners

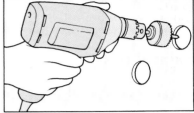

2 Bore holes for ducting with a hole saw

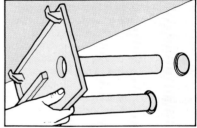

3 Pass both ducts through the wall

4 Plug gaps around ducts with insulation

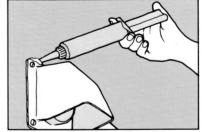

5 Seal edge of duct covers with caulk

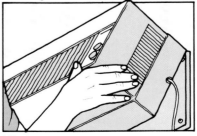

6 Fit the ventilator unit on the inside

VENTILATORS

Mounting a flush ventilator

Most flush-mounted ventilators require a wooden frame to line a hole cut through the wall. Make it to the dimensions supplied by the manufacturer of the ventilator. Construct the frame with lap joints or glued and screwed butt joints. Decide on the approximate position of the unit, then locate the wall studs to align one with the side of the unit. Mark the rectangle for the wooden lining onto the wall, then drill through the plasterboard at the corners of the outline. Cut out the rectangle with a keyhole saw or saber saw. Cut and remove the wall insulation. Working from outside, cut away the siding and sheathing along the same lines. Saw off any studs obstructing the hole flush with its edges. (Do not remove studs from a bearing wall without consulting a building inspector.)

Insert the lining. The ventilator must be angled downwards a few degrees towards the outside to drain away condensation. If this angle is built into the ventilator unit, the wooden lining can be set flush with the wall, otherwise tilt it a fraction by shimming it underneath before nailing. Measure the diagonals to make sure the lining is square in the hole.

Fit the main unit in the liner and screw it to the front edge of the lining. Fit the front panel onto the unit. Outside, seal the seams between the sheathing, lining and unit with caulk.

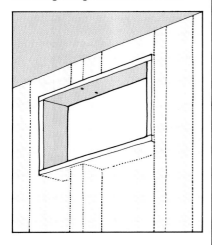

Mounting a flush ventilator
Fit a wooden liner in the wall close to the ceiling where it will be in the best position to extract hot, rising air. Screw the ventilator to the front edge of the liner.

FITTING A UNIT IN A MASONRY WALL

Decide on the approximate position of the unit, then mark its position on the wall by scribing around it with a pencil or awl. Use a masonry drill to bore a hole through the wall at each corner, then chop along the plaster between them with a bricklayer's chisel. Drill further holes around the perimeter of the hole and chop out the masonry with a cold chisel. Remove the whole bricks by drilling out the mortar joints. After cutting halfway through the wall, finish the hole from the outside.

Mounting a ventilator liner ▶
Cut a rectangular hole through the masonry. Construct a wood liner using butt joints at the corners. Insert the liner, tilting it slightly toward the outside if necessary.

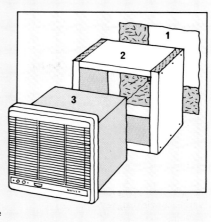

DEHUMIDIFIERS CONTROL CONDENSATION

To combat condensation you can remove the moisture-laden air by ventilation or warm it so that it can carry more water vapor before it becomes saturated. An alternative measure is to extract the water itself from the air using a dehumidifier. This is achieved by drawing air from the room into the unit and passing it over cold coils upon which water vapor condenses and drips into a reservoir. The cold but now dry air is drawn by a fan over heated coils before being returned to the room as additional convected heat.

The process is based on the refrigeration principle that gas under pressure heats up and when the pressure drops, so does the temperature of the gas. In a dehumidifier, a compressor delivers pressurized gas to the "hot" coils, in turn leading to the larger "cold" coils, which allow the gas to expand. The cooled gas returns to the compressor for recycling.

A dehumidifier for domestic use is built into a cabinet which resembles a large hi-fi speaker. It contains a humidistat, which automatically switches on the unit when the moisture content of the air reaches a predetermined level. When the reservoir is full, the machine shuts down to prevent overflow and an indicator lights up to remind you to empty the water in the container.

When installed in a damp room, a dehumidifier will extract excess moisture from the furnishings and fabric of the building in a week or two. After that it will monitor the moisture content of the air to maintain a stabilized atmosphere. A portable version can be wheeled from room to room, where it is plugged into a standard wall stocket.

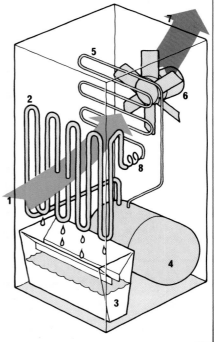

The working components of a dehumidifier ▶
The diagram illustrates the layout of a typical domestic dehumidifier.
1 Incoming damp air
2 Cold coils
3 Water reservoir
4 Compressor
5 Hot coils
6 Fan
7 Dry, warm air
8 Capillary tube where gas expands

AIR CONDITIONERS

Central air-conditioning systems should be checked once a year in early spring by a professional service technician. During the air-conditioning season, the homeowner should check and replace the filters once each month, or more frequently in dusty areas.

Even small window- or wall-mounted air conditioners are mostly factory-sealed and lubricated. However, it is important to keep the indoor and outdoor grillework dust-free to maintain optimum cooling efficiency and to prevent overstraining various components. Vacuum the front of the unit frequently. Once a year, remove the cover and vacuum behind it.

How air conditioning works

An air conditioner works on the same refrigeration principle described for a dehumidifier and incorporates similar gas-filled coils and a compressor. However, airflow within the unit is different. Individual units are divided into separate compartments within one cabinet. Room air is drawn into the cooling compartment and passed over the evaporation coils which absorb heat before a fan returns the air to the room at a lower temperature. As moisture vapor condenses on the coils, the unit also acts as a dehumidifier, a welcome bonus in hot, humid weather. Condensed water is normally drained to the outside of the house.

Gas in the evaporation coils moves on, carrying absorbed heat to the compartment facing the outside, where it is radiated from the condenser coils and blown outside by a fan.

A thermostat operates a valve, which reverses the flow of refrigerant when the temperature in the room drops below the setting. The system is automatic so that the unit can heat the room if it is cold in the early morning. As the sun rises and boosts the temperature, the air conditioner switches over to maintain a constant temperature indoors.

Choose a unit with variable fan speed and a method for directing the chilled air where it will be most effective in cooling the whole room. Usually this is at ceiling level, where the cold air falls slowly over the whole room area.

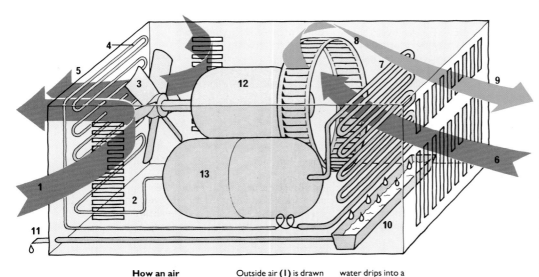

How an air conditioner works
The diagram shows the mechanism of a small wall-mounted or window-mounted air conditioner but it illustrates the principle employed by all air conditioners.

Outside air (**1**) is drawn through the side vents (**2**) by fan (**3**) which blows it over the hot coils (**4**). The air extracts heat from the coils and takes it outside (**5**). Warm, humid air from the interior (**6**) is drawn over the cold coils (**7**) by a centrifugal fan (**8**) and returned to the room cooled and dry (**9**). The condensed

water drips into a reservoir (**10**) and drains to the outside (**11**). The motor (**12**) powers the fans and compressor (**13**), which pumps gas around the system.

CHOOSING THE CAPACITY

To reduce the running costs of an air conditioner, try to match its capacity—the amount of heat it can absorb—to the size of the room it will be cooling. A unit which is too small will be running most of the time without complete success, while one that is much too large will chill the air so quickly that it won't be able to remove much moisture vapor, so the atmosphere may still feel uncomfortable when it is humid. Ideally, the unit should be working flat-out on only the hottest of days.

The capacity of a conditioner is measured in British Thermal Units (BTU). A unit with a capacity of 9000 BTU will remove the amount of heat every hour. As a rough guide to capacity, find the volume of the area you wish to cool (length × width × height), then allow 5 BTU per cubic foot. Ask the supplier to provide a more accurate calculation which will take into consideration other factors such as size and number of windows, insulation and heat-generating equipment in the room.

MOUNTING THE UNIT

Cut a hole through the wall and fit a wooden lining as for a heat-exchanging ventilator. Being a larger and heavier unit, an air conditioner will have some sort of supporting cage or metal brackets.

Units designed for installing in windows are supplied with adjustable frames and weatherstripping. After attaching the frame to the window opening, the conditioner is lifted into the window, then slid into place.

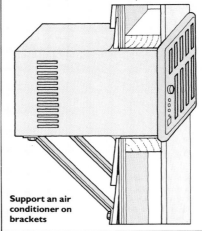

Support an air conditioner on brackets

BUILDING CODES AND PERMITS

Building codes

Building codes are comprehensive guidelines intended to set standards for construction practices and material specifications. Their purpose is to ensure the adequate structural and mechanical performance, fire safety and overall quality of buildings and to address health and environmental concerns related to the way buildings are constructed. By setting minimum standards, building codes also limit unfair competitive practices among contractors.

Building codes address nearly every detail of building construction from the acceptable recipes for concrete used in the foundation to the permissible fire rating of the roof finish material—and many features in between. Partly because codes attempt to be as comprehensive as possible and also because they must address different concerns in varied locales, they are very lengthy, complex and lack uniformity from region to region. A further complication is that many new building products become available each year that are not accounted for in existing codes. Model codes promulgated by four major organizations are widely used for reference throughout the United States.

The Uniform Building Code, published by the International Conference of Building Officials, is perhaps the most widely accepted code. ICBO republishes the entire code every three years and publishes revisions annually. A short form of the Uniform Building Code covering buildings with less than three stories and less than 6,000 square feet of ground floor area is available—easier for home builders, and remodelers' reference.

The BOCA-Basic Building Code, issued by the Building Officials and Code Administrators International, Inc., is also widely used. An abridged form designed for residential construction, which includes plumbing and wiring standards, is available.

A third model code, prepared under the supervision of the American Insurance Association and known as the National Building Code, serves as the basis for codes adopted by many communities. It, too, is available in a short form for matters related to home construction.

The Standard Building Code is published by the Southern Building Code Congress International, Inc. It addresses conditions and problems prevalent in the southern United States.

While it is likely that one of the model codes named above serves as the basis for the building code in your community, municipal governments and states frequently add standards and restrictions. It is your local building department that ultimately decides what is acceptable and what is not. Consult that agency if a code question should arise.

Building codes are primarily designed for the safety of the building occupants and the general welfare of the community at large. It is wise to follow *all* practices outlined by the prevailing code in your area.

Building permits

A building permit is generally required for new construction, remodeling projects that involve structural changes or additions, and major demolition projects. In some locales it may be necessary to obtain a building permit for constructing in-ground pools, and you may need a building permit or rigger's license to erect scaffolding as an adjunct to nonstructural work on a house.

To obtain a building permit, you must file forms prescribed by your local building department that answer questions about the proposed site and project. In addition, it is necessary to file a complete set of drawings of the project along with detailed specifications. A complete set normally includes a plot plan or survey, foundation plan, floor plans, wall sections and electrical, plumbing and mechanical plans. Building permit fees are usually assessed based on the estimated cost of construction and records of the application are usually passed along to the local tax department for reassessment of the property value.

At the time you apply for a building permit, you may be advised of other applications for official permission that are required. For example, you may need to apply to the county health department concerning projects that may affect sewerage facilities and natural water supplies. It is important to arrange inspections in a timely way since finish stages cannot proceed until the structural, electrical, plumbing and mechanical work are approved.

Anyone may apply for a building permit, but it is usually best to have an architect or contractor file in your behalf, even if you plan to do the work yourself.

Zoning restrictions

Even for projects that do not require a building permit, local zoning regulations may limit the scope and nature of the construction permitted. Whereas building codes and permit regulations relate to a building itself, zoning rules address the needs and conditions of the community as a whole by regulating the development and uses of property. Zoning restrictions may apply to such various cases as whether a single-family house can be remodeled into apartments, whether a commercial space can be converted to residential use or the permissible height of a house or outbuilding.

It is advisable to apply to the local zoning board for approval before undertaking any kind of construction or remodeling that involves a house exterior or yard or if the project will substantially change the way a property is used. If the project does not conform with the standing zoning guidelines, you may apply to the zoning board for a variance. It is best to enlist the help of an architect or attorney for this.

Landmark regulations

Homes in historic districts may be subject to restrictions placed to help the neighborhood retain its architectural distinction and character. For the most part in designated landmark areas, changes in house exteriors are closely regulated. While extensive remodeling that would significantly change the architectural style are almost never permitted, even seemingly small modifications of existing structures are scrutinized. For example, metal or vinyl replacement windows may not be permitted for Victorian homes in designated areas, or the exterior paint and roof colors may be subject to approval. Even the color of the mortar used to repoint brickwork may be specified by the local landmarks commission or similar regulating body. Designs for new construction must conform to the prevalent architectural character. If you live in an historic district, it is advised that you apply to the governing body for approval of any plans for exterior renovation.

SEE ALSO

Details for: ▷

Official permission   74

73

WILL YOU NEED A PERMIT OR VARIANCE?

Building code requirements and zoning regulations vary from city to city and frequently have county and state restrictions added to them. For this reason, it is impossible to state categorically which home-improvement projects require official permission and which do not. The chart below, which lists some of the most frequently undertaken projects, is meant to serve as a rough guide. Taken as a whole, it suggests a certain logic for anticipating when and what type of approval may be needed. Whether or not official approval is required, all work should be carried out in conformity with local code standards.

TYPE OF WORK	BUILDING PERMIT NEEDED		ZONING APPROVAL NEEDED	
 Exterior painting and repairs Interior decoration and repairs	NO	Permit or rigger's license may be needed to erect exterior scaffolding	NO	Certificate of appropriateness may be needed in historic areas
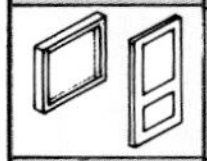 Replacing windows and doors	NO		NO	Permissible styles may be restricted in historic districts
 Electrical	NO	Have work performed or checked by a licensed contractor	NO	Outdoor lighting may be subject to approval
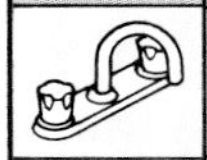 Plumbing	NO	Have work performed or checked by a licensed contractor	NO	Work involving new water supply, septic or sewerage systems may require county health department
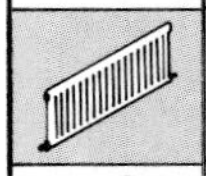 Heating	NO		NO	Installation of new oil storage tanks may require state environmental agency approval
 Constructing patios and decks	Possibly		Possibly	
Installing a hot tub	NO		NO	
 Structural alterations	YES		NO	Unless alterations change building height above limit or proximity of building to lot line
 Attic remodeling	NO	Ascertain whether joists can safely support the floor load	NO	
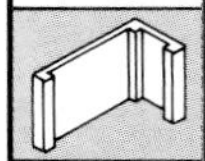 Building a fence or garden wall	NO		YES	In cases where structure is adjacent to public road or easement or extends above a height set by board
 Planting a hedge	NO		NO	
 Path or sidewalk paving	NO		Possibly	Public sidewalks must conform to local standards and specifications
 Clearing land	NO		YES	County and state environmental approval may also be needed
 Constructing an in-ground pool	YES		YES	County and state environmental approval may also be needed
 Constructing outbuildings	YES	For buildings larger than set limit	Possibly	
 Adding a porch	NO	Unless larger than set limit	Possibly	Regulations often set permissible setback from public road
 Adding a sunspace or greenhouse	YES		Possibly	Yes, if local rules apply to extensions
 Constructing a garage	YES		Possibly	Yes, if used for a commercial vehicle and within set proximity to lot line
 Driveway paving	NO		Possibly	Yes where access to public road created, also restrictions on proximity to lot lines
 Constructing a house extension	YES		Possibly	Regulations may limit permissible house size and proximity to lot lines
 Demolition	YES	If work involves structural elements	NO	Structures in historic districts may be protected by regulations
 Converting 1-family house to multi-unit dwelling	YES	Fire safety and ventilation codes are frequently more stringent for multiple dwellings	YES	
 Converting a residential building to commercial use	YES		YES	

BUILDER'S TOOL KIT

Bricklayers, carpenters and plasterers are all specialist builders, each requiring a set of specific tools, but the amateur is more like one of the self-employed builders who must be able to tackle several areas of building work, and so need a much wider range of tools than the specialist. The builder's tool kit suggested here is for renovating and improving the structure of a house and for erecting and restoring garden structures or paving.

LEVELING AND MEASURING TOOLS

You can make several specialized tools for measuring and leveling, but don't skimp on essentials like a good level and a strong tape measure.

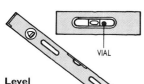

Level
A level is a machine-made straightedge incorporating special glass tubes, or vials, that contain a liquid. In each vial an air bubble floats. When a bubble rests exactly between two lines marked on the glass, the structure on which the level is held is known to be exactly horizontal or vertical, depending on the vial's orientation. Buy a wooden or lightweight aluminum level 2 to 3 feet long. A well-made one is very strong, but treat it with care and always clean mortar or plaster from it before the material sets.

VIAL

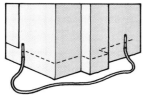

Water level
You can make a water level from a garden hose with short lengths of transparent plastic tube plugged into its ends. Fill the hose with water until it appears in both tubes. As water level is constant, the levels in the tubes are always identical and so can be used for marking identical heights even over long distances and around obstacles and bends.

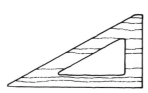

Builder's square
A large set square is useful when you set out brick or concrete-block corners. The best ones are stamped out of sheet metal, but you can make a serviceable one by cutting out a thick plywood right-angled triangle with a hypotenuse of about 2 feet 6 inches. Cut out the center of the triangle to reduce the weight.

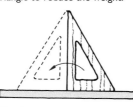

Checking a square
Accuracy is important, so check the square by placing it against a straight strip of wood on the floor, drawing a line against the square to make a right angle with the strip, then turning the square to see if it forms the same angle from the other side.

Try square
Use a try square for marking out square cuts or joints on timber.

Making a plumb line
Any small but heavy weight hung on a length of line or string will make a suitable plumb line for judging the verticality of structures or surfaces.

Bricklayer's line
Use a bricklayer's line as a guide for laying bricks or blocks level. It is a length of nylon string stretched between two flat-bladed pins that are driven into vertical joints at the ends of a wall. There are also special line blocks that hook over the bricks at the ends of a course. As an improvisation, you can stretch a string between two stakes driven into the ground outside the line of the wall.

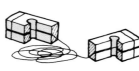

Line blocks
Blocks grip the brickwork corners; the line passes through their slots.

Plasterer's rule
A plasterer's rule is simply a straight wooden strip used for scraping plaster and rendering undercoats level.

Straightedge
Any length of straight, fairly stout lumber can be used to tell whether a surface is flat or, used with a level, to test whether two points are at the same height.

Gauge stick
For gauging the height of brick courses, calibrate a wooden strip by making saw cuts across it at 3-inch intervals—the thickness of a brick plus its mortar joint.

Tape measure
An ordinary retractable steel tape measure is adequate for most purposes, but if you need to mark out or measure a large plot, rent a wind-up tape up to 100 feet in length.

Marking gauge
This tool has a sharp steel point for scoring a line on lumber parallel to its edge. Its adjustable stock acts as a fence and keeps the point a constant distance from the edge.

FLOATS AND TROWELS

For professional builders, floats and trowels have specific uses, but in home maintenance, the small trowel for repointing brickwork is often ideal for patching small areas of plaster, while the plasterer's trowel is as likely to be used for smoothing concrete.

Brick trowel
A brick trowel is for handling and placing mortar when laying bricks or concrete blocks. A professional might use one with a blade as long as 1 foot, but such a trowel is too heavy and unwieldy for the amateur, so buy a good-quality brick trowel with a short blade.

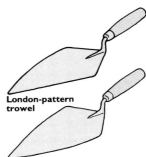

London-pattern trowel

Canadian-pattern trowel

The blade of a *London-pattern trowel* has one curved edge for cutting bricks, a skill that requires much practice to perfect. The blade's other edge is straight, for picking up mortar. This type of trowel is made in right- and left-handed versions, so buy the correct one. A right-handed trowel has its curved edge on the right when you point it away from you.

A *Canadian-pattern trowel* is symmetrical, enabling both left- and right-handed people to use it.

Pointing trowel
The blade of a pointing trowel is no more than 3 to 4 inches long, designed for repairing or shaping mortar joints between bricks.

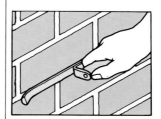

Pointer
A pointer is shaped for making 'V' or concave joints between bricks. The narrow blade is dragged along the mortar joint and the curved front end is used to shape the verticals.

Frenchman
A Frenchman is a specialized tool for cutting excess mortar away from brickwork jointing. You can make one by heating and bending an old table knife.

Continental-pattern trowels

Using a pointing tray
A pointing tray makes the filling of mortar joints very easy. Place the flat lip of the tray just under a horizontal joint and scrape the mortar into place with a jointer. Turn the tray around and push mortar into vertical joints through the gap between the raised sides.

• **Essential tools**
Brick trowel
Pointing trowel
Plasterer's trowel
Mortar board
Hawk
Level
Try square
Plumb line

Wooden float

A wooden float is for applying and smoothing stucco and concrete to a fine, attractive texture. The more expensive ones have detachable handles so that their wooden blades can be replaced when they wear. But the amateur is unlikely to use a float often enough to justify the cost of buying one.

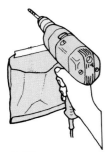

Drilling masonry for wall plugs

Set the drill for low speed and hammer action, and wrap tape around the bit to mark the depth to be drilled. Allow for slightly more depth than the length of the plug, as dust will pack down into the hole when you insert it. Drill the hole in stages.

Protect floor coverings and paintwork from falling dust by taping a paper bag under the position of the hole before you start drilling.

• **Essential tools**
  Straightedge
  Tape measure
  Claw hammer
  Light sledgehammer
  Panel saw
  Tenon saw
  Hacksaw
  Padsaw
  Power drill
  Masonry bits
  Brace and bit

76

Plasterer's trowel

A plasterer's trowel is a steel float for applying plaster and stucco to walls. It is also dampened and used for "polishing," stroking the surface of the material when it has firmed up. Some builders prefer to apply stucco with a heavy trowel and finish it with a more flexible blade, but one has to be quite skilled to exploit such subtle differences.

DRILLS

A powerful electric drill is invaluable to a builder, but a hand brace is useful when you have to bore holes outdoors or in attics and cellars that lack convenient electric sockets.

Power drill

Buy a power drill, a range of twist drills and some spade or power-bore bits for drilling lumber. Make sure that the tool has a percussion or hammer action for drilling masonry. For masonry you need special drill bits tipped with tungsten carbide. The smaller ones are matched to the size of standard wall plugs, though there are much larger ones with reduced shanks that can be used in a standard power-drill chuck. The larger bits are expensive, so rent them when you need them. Percussion bits are even tougher than masonry bits, with shatterproof tips.

Brace and bit

A brace and bit is the ideal hand tool for drilling large holes in lumber, and when fitted with a screwdriver bit, it gives good leverage for driving or extracting large woodscrews.

BOARDS FOR CARRYING MORTAR OR PLASTER

Any convenient-sized sheet of ½- or ¾-inch exterior-grade plywood can be used as a mixing board for plaster or mortar. A panel about 3 feet square is ideal, and a smaller spotboard, about 2 feet square, is convenient for carrying the material to the actual work site. In either case, screw some wood strips to the undersides of the boards to make them easier to lift and carry. Make a small, lightweight hawk for carrying pointing mortar or plaster by nailing a single strip underneath a plywood board so that you can plug a handle into it.

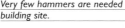
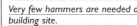

A homemade hawk

HAMMERS

Very few hammers are needed on a building site.

Claw hammer

Choose a strong claw hammer for building wooden stud partitions, nailing floorboards, making door and window frames and putting up fencing.

Light sledgehammer

A light sledgehammer is used for driving cold chisels and for various demolition jobs. It is also useful for driving large masonry nails into walls.

Sledgehammer

Rent a big sledgehammer if you have to break up concrete or paving. It's also the best tool for driving stakes or fence posts into the ground, though you can make do with a light sledge if the ground is not too hard.

Mallet

A carpenter's wooden mallet is the proper tool for driving wood chisels, but you can use a hammer if the chisels have impact-resistant plastic handles.

SAWS

Every builder needs a range of handsaws, but consider renting a power saw when you have to cut a lot of heavy structural timbers, and especially if you plan to rip floorboards down to width, a very tiring job when done by hand.

There are special power saws for cutting metal, and even for sawing through masonry.

Panel saw

All kinds of man-made building boards are used in house construction, so buy a good panel saw—useful also for cutting large structural timbers to the required lengths.

Tenon saw

A tenon saw accurately cuts wall studs, floorboards, paneling and joints. Metal stiffening along the top of the blade keeps it rigid and less likely to go off line.

Padsaw

Also called a keyhole saw, this small saw has a narrow tapered blade for cutting holes in wood.

Coping saw

A coping saw has a frame that holds a fairly coarse but very narrow blade under tension for cutting curves in wood.

Floorboard saw

If you pry a floorboard above its neighbors you can cut across it with an ordinary tenon saw. But a floorboard saw's curved cutting edge makes it easier to avoid damaging the board on either side.

Hacksaw

The hardened-steel blades of a hacksaw have fine teeth for cutting metal. Use one to cut steel concrete-reinforcing rods or small pieces of sheet metal.

Sheet saw

A hacksaw's frame makes it unsuitable for cutting large sheets of metal. For that job, bolt a hacksaw blade to the edge of the flat blade of a sheet saw, which will also cut corrugated plastic sheeting and roofing slates.

Universal saw

A universal or general-purpose saw is designed to cut wood, metal, plastics and building boards. Its short frameless blade has a low-friction coating and is stiff enough to make straight cuts without wandering. The handle can be set at various angles. The saw is particularly useful for cutting secondhand lumber, which may contain nails or screws that would blunt an ordinary saw.

Masonry saw

A masonry saw looks much like a wood handsaw but its tungsten-carbide teeth cut brick, concrete blocks and stone.

POWER SAWS

A *circular saw* will accurately rip lumber or man-made boards down to size. As well as doing away with the effort of hand-sawing large timbers, a sharp power saw produces such a clean cut that there is often no need for planing afterwards.

A *power jigsaw* cuts curves in lumber and sheet materials but is also useful for cutting holes in fixed wall panels and sawing through floorboards so as to lift them.

A *reciprocating saw* is a two-handed power saw with a long pointed blade, powerful enough to cut through heavy timber sections and even through a complete stud partition, panels and all.

GLAZIER'S TOOLS

Glass is such a hard and brittle material that it can be worked only with specialized tools.

Glass cutter
A glass cutter doesn't really cut glass but scores a line in it. The scoring is done by a tiny hardened-steel wheel or a chip of industrial diamond mounted in the penlike holder. The glass will break along the scored line when pressure is applied to it.

Beam compass cutter
A beam compass cutter is for scoring circles on glass—when, for example, you need a round hole in a window pane to fit a ventilator. The cutting wheel is mounted at the end of an adjustable beam that turns on a center pivot which is fixed to the glass by suction.

Spear-point glass drill
A glass drill has a flat spearhead-shaped tip of tungsten-steel shaft. The shape of the tip reduces friction that would otherwise crack the glass, but it needs lubricating with oil, paraffin or water during drilling.

Hacking knife
A hacking knife has a heavy steel blade for chipping old putty out of window rabbets so as to remove the glass. Place its point between the putty and the frame and tap its thickened back with a hammer.

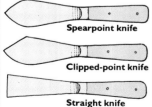

Spearpoint knife

Clipped-point knife

Straight knife

Putty knife
The blunt blade of a putty knife is for shaping and smoothing fresh putty. You can choose between spearpoint, clipped-point and straight blades according to your personal preference.

CHISELS

As well as chisels for cutting and paring wood joints, you will need some special ones for masonry work.

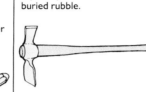

Cold chisel
Cold chisels are made from solid steel hexagonal-section rod. They are primarily for cutting metal bars and chopping the heads off rivets, but a builder will use one for cutting a chase in plaster and brickwork or chopping out old brick pointing.

Slip a plastic safety sleeve over the chisel to protect your hand from a misplaced blow with the sledgehammer.

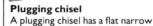

Plugging chisel
A plugging chisel has a flat narrow bit (tip) for cutting out old pointing. It's worth renting one if you have a large area of brickwork to repoint.

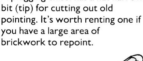

Bricklayer's chisel
The wide bit of a bricklayer's chisel is for cutting bricks and concrete blocks. It's also useful for levering up floorboards.

WORK GLOVES

Wear strong work gloves whenever you carry paving stones, concrete blocks or rough lumber. Ordinary gardening gloves are better than none but won't last long on a building site. The best work gloves have leather palms and fingers, though you may prefer a pair with ventilated backs for comfort in hot weather.

DIGGING TOOLS

Much building work requires some kind of digging—for laying strip foundations and concrete pads, sinking rows of postholes and so on. You may already have the essential tools in your garden shed; others you can rent.

Pickaxe
Use a medium-weight pickaxe to break up heavily compacted soil, especially if it contains a lot of buried rubble.

Mattlock
The wide blade of a mattock is ideal for breaking up heavy clay soil, and it's better than an ordinary pickaxe for ground that's riddled with tree roots.

Spade
Buy a good-quality spade for excavating soil and mixing concrete. One with a stainless-steel blade is best, but alloy steel will last fairly well if it is looked after. For strength choose a D-shaped handle whose hardwood shaft has been split and riveted with metal plates to the crosspiece, and make sure that the shaft socket and blade are forged in one piece.

Square blades seem to be the most popular, though some builders prefer a round-mouth spade with a long pole handle for digging deep trenches and holes.

Shovel
You can use a spade for mixing and placing concrete or mortar, but the raised edges of a shovel retain it better.

Garden rake
Use an ordinary garden rake to spread gravel or level wet concrete, but be sure to wash it before any concrete sets on it.

Posthole auger
Rent a posthole auger to sink narrow holes for fence and gate posts by driving it into the ground like a corkscrew and pulling out plugs of earth.

Wheelbarrow
The average garden wheelbarrow is not really strong enough for work on building sites, which entails carrying heavy loads of wet concrete and rubble. Unless the tubular underframe is rigidly strutted, the barrow's thin metal body will distort and perhaps spill its load as you cross rough ground. Check, too, that the axle is fixed securely. Cheap wheelbarrows often lose their wheels when their loads are being tipped into excavations.

SCREWDRIVERS

One's choice of screwdrivers is a personal matter, and most people accumulate a collection of types and sizes over the years.

Cabinet screwdriver
Buy at least one large flat-tip screwdriver. The fixed variety is quite adequate but a pump-action one, which drives large screws very quickly, is useful when you assemble big wooden building structures.

Phillips-head screwdriver
Choose the size and type of Phillips-head screwdriver to suit the work at hand. There is no most useful size as the driver must fit the screw slots exactly.

PLANES

Your choice of planes depends on the kind of joinery you plan to do. Sophisticated framing may call for molding or grooving planes, but most woodwork needs only skimming to leave a fairly smooth finish.

Jack plane
A medium-size bench plane, the jack plane, is the best general-purpose tool.

ADDITIONAL BUILDER'S TOOLS

Crowbar
A crowbar, or wrecking bar, is for demolishing timber framework. Force the flat tip between components and use the leverage of the long shaft to pry them apart. Choose a bar that has a claw at one end for removing large nails.

Mastic guns
Nonsetting mastic is for sealing gaps between masonry and wooden frames as well as other joints between materials whose different rates of expansion will eventually cause them to crack and eject a rigid filler. Mastic comes in squeeze tubes, but is easier to apply from a cartridge in a spring-loaded gun.

• **Essential tools**
Glass cutter
Putty knife
Cold chisel
Bricklayer's chisel
Spade
Shovel
Rake
Wheelbarrow
Cabinet screwdriver
Phillips-head screwdriver
Jack plane

A

Aggregate
Particles of sand or stone mixed with cement and water to make concrete or added to paint to make a textured finish.

Alkali-resistant primer
A primer used to prevent the alkali content of some building materials from attacking subsequent coats of paint.

B

Balanced flue
A ducting system that allows a heating appliance, such as a boiler, to draw fresh air from, and discharge gases to, the outside of a building.

Ballast
Naturally occurring sand and gravel mix used as *aggregate* for making concrete.

Batt
A short, cut length of fiberglass or mineral-fiber insulating material.

Blown
To have broken away, as when a layer of cement *stucco* has parted from a wall.

C

Cavity wall
A wall consisting of two separate masonry skins with an air space between them.

Condensation
Air-borne moisture that liquefies on a surface that is cooler than the air.

D

Damp-proof course (DPC)
A layer of impervious material that prevents moisture from rising from the ground into the walls of a building.

Damp-proof membrane (DPM)
A layer of impervious material that prevents moisture from rising through a concrete floor; a *vapor barrier*.

Drip groove
A groove cut or molded in the underside of a door or windowsill to prevent rainwater from running back to the wall.

E

Eaves
The overhang of a roof past the building's outer walls.

Efflorescence
A white powdery deposit caused by soluble salts migrating to the surface of *masonry*.

External wall insulation
Thermal insulating material that is fixed to the outer surface of a house in order to prevent transmission of heat to the outside.

F

Fascia board
A strip of wood that covers the ends of *rafters* and to which external guttering is fixed.

Flashing
A weatherproof junction between a roof and a wall or chimney, or between one roof and another.

Furring strips
Parallel strips of wood fixed to a wall or ceiling to provide a framework for attaching panels.

G

Galvanized
Covered with a protective coating of zinc.

Glazing
The glass or plastic panes in a window.

H

Heave
An upward swelling of the ground caused by excess moisture.

Hydraulic cement
A specially formulated cement used to patch cracks that are active water leaks.

I

Insulation
Materials used to reduce the transmission of heat or sound; or, nonconductive material surrounding electrical wires or connections to prevent the passage of electricity.

J

Jamb
The vertical side member of a door or window frame; sometimes, the frame as a whole.

L

Lath and plaster
A method of finishing a stud-framed wall or ceiling in which narrow strips of wood are nailed to the studs or joists to provide a supporting framework for plaster.

M

Masonry
Bricks, stones, and concrete blocks used as construction materials.

Mastic
A nonsetting compound used to seal joints.

Mono-pitch roof
A roof that slopes in one direction only.

P

Paint stripper
A chemical that softens old paint so that it can be removed from a surface.

Pitch
The incline of a roof expressed as a ratio of its vertical rise to twice its horizontal run, thereby taking into account both sides of the roof. See also *Slope*.

Primer
The first coat of a paint system applied to protect a workpiece and reduce the absorption of subsequent coats.

R

Rafter
One of a set of parallel sloping beams that form the main structural element of a roof.

S

Sash
The openable part of a window.

Scratchcoat
The bottom layer of cement *stucco*.

Screed
A straight 2 x 4 used to level and compact concrete; or, to level and compact concrete using a straight 2 x 4.

Sealer
A primary coating applied to masonry surfaces that forms a base for subsequent coats of paint.

Service panel
The point at which the main electrical service cable connects to the house circuits. Circuit breakers in the panel protect individual circuits in the system. In older homes, the service panel is a fuse box, whose fuses serve the same purpose as circuit breakers.

Sill
The lowest horizontal member of a door or window frame; or, the lowest horizontal member of a stud partition.

Slab floor
A concrete slab laid on a substratum of gravel in a basement.

Slope
The incline of a roof expressed as a ratio of the roof's vertical rise to the horizontal run of one side. See also *Pitch*.

Soffit
The underside of a part of a building, such as the eaves or an archway.

Spalling
Flaking of the outer face of masonry caused by expanding moisture in icy conditions.

Stile
A vertical side member of a door or window *sash*.

Stucco
A thin layer of cement-based mortar applied to exterior walls to provide a protective finish. Sometimes, fine stone aggregate is embedded in the mortar. Or, to apply cement-based mortar.

Sump pump
A pump that expels excess water in a perpetually damp basement.

T

Thinner
A solvent used to dilute paint or varnish.

Thixotropic
Term used to describe paints that have a jelly-like consistency until stirred or applied, at which point they become liquefied.

Top coat
The outer layer of a paint system.

U

Undercoat
A layer of paint used to obliterate the color of a primer and to build a protective body of paint prior to the application of a top coat.

Underlayment
The heavy asphalt-saturated felt paper under roofing that prevents the passage of moisture but not of vapor.

V

Vapor barrier
A layer of impervious material that prevents the passage of moisture.

W

Warp
To bend or twist as a result of damp or heat.

Water-resistant wallboard
Wall panels made for use in damp locations like bathrooms and kitchens; also called dry-wall.

Weatherstripping
A special molding fitted at the bottom of an exterior door to prevent the passage of moisture and the flow of air underneath.

Weep hole
A small hole at the base of a *cavity wall* designed to allow absorbed water to drain to the outside.